# Chomsky's Internalist View of Language

# Chomsky's Internalist View of Language

## — A Critical Survey —

Kanya Sen Gupta

shakti publications
empowering through books

**Cataloging in Publication Data — DK**
[Courtesy: D.K. Agencies (P) Ltd. <docinfo@dkagencies.com>]

**Sen Gupta, Kanya, author.**
Chomsky's internalist view of language : a critical survey / Kanya Sen Gupta.
pages cm
Includes bibliographical references and index.
ISBN 9788194622161

1. Chomsky, Noam. 2. Language and languages – Philosophy. 3. Internalism (Theory of knowledge) I. Title.

LCC P106.S46 2022 | DDC 401 23

ISBN 978-81-946221-6-1
First published in India 2022


*Printed and published by*:
Shakti Publications
797/64 (2nd floor), Lekhu Nagar
Tri nagar, Delhi - 110035
*Mob.*: 9953680097
*e-mail*: pub.shakti@gmail.com

*Distributed by:*
D.K. Printworld (P) Ltd.
*Regd. Office:* "Vedaśrī", F-395, Sudarshan Park
(Metro Station: ESI Hospital), New Delhi - 110015
*Phones*: (011) 2545 3975, 2546 6019
*e-mail*: indology@dkprintworld.com
*Website*: www.dkprintworld.com

In loving memory
of my affectionate Dida
**Usharani Dasgupta**
who, I believe,
is still with me

# Preface

In this book, I have critically analysed the following:

Chomsky's preference for mentalism, his emphasis that rules of language are mentally represented, or that native speakers have unconscious knowledge of rules of language. And from this, Chomsky's jump to the conclusion about the privacy of language. Next is his emphasis on competence (knowledge of language) as opposed to performance and creativity of language. Further, Chomskey's account of unconscious knowledge of language. Finally, his innateness hypothesis.

I am grateful to my teacher Dr Soumitra Basu, Professor of Philosophy, Jadavpur University as well as to my father Dr Kalyan Sengupta, former Professor of Philosophy, Jadavpur University for their interest in this book. Also, many thanks are due to my teacher David E. Cooper, Emeritus Professor of University of Durham, England and his book *Knowledge of Language* which enabled me to further my knowledge of language. I must also be grateful to my mother, Dr. Ananya Sengupta for inspiring me to engage in this book.

Last but not the least, I am very much grateful to Mrs Varsha Goyal of Shakti Publications for taking up this book for publishing.

# Contents

# 1

# Chomsky's Mentalism

CHOMSKY starts from a fact about language which according to him is the central fact to which any significant theory must address itself (Chomsky 1964: 51). The central fact is the creative aspect of language or the ability of the native speaker to produce and understand sentences not encountered before. Chomsky emphatically points out that a theory of language that neglects this creative aspect of language is of only marginal interest. He often talks about the speaker's ability to produce new sentences, sentences that are immediately understood by other speakers although they bear no physical resemblance to sentences which are familiar. And Chomsky's thesis of mentalism is specifically addressed to the linguistic creativity. But mentalism, it should be noted, is only a later development in Chomsky's writings on language.

This is not to say that his earlier works do not indicate any inclination towards mentalism. For example, his thoroughgoing criticism of reinforcement theory, etc. in his review of B.F. Skinner, *Verbal Behaviour* (1959) surely reflects his preference for mentalism. This is only to highlight that Chomsky in his later works, *Aspects of the Theory of Syntax* (1965), *Cartesian Linguistics* (1966) and *Language and Mind* (1968), began to emphasize that the rules of language are mentally represented, or that native speakers have unconscious knowledge of language or rules.

Chomsky holds that this tacit knowledge or normal mastery of language explains the creativity of language.

> Normal mastery of a language involves ... the ability to understand immediately an indefinite number of sentences .... .
> – Chomsky 1964: 51

In other words, since one has tacit or unconscious knowledge of rules (competence), one can produce and understand sentences not encountered before.

Now empiricists like Leonard Bloomfield, W.O. Quine and others may retort that even if we accept creativity of language, there is no reason to account for it in terms of inner knowledge of language. In fact, this creativity can be explained by the strategy of arguing from analogy:

> It is evident how new sentences may be built from old materials and volunteered on appropriate occasions simply by virtue of analogies. – Quine 1960, 275: 9; Bloomfield 1935: 275

This is done on the basis of inductive generalization from what we learn in the past and applying the generalization to the new sentences, e.g. "He reads," etc. because they are observably similar to such sentences as "He speaks", "He rides", etc. – sentences that one has already learned as grammatical. But Chomsky will not accept this. His point is:

> Knowledge of language cannot arise by application of step by step inductive operations (segmentation, classification, substitution procedures, analogy, association, conditioning and so on) of any sort that have been developed within linguistics.
> – 1974: 128

And further:

> ... We must attribute to the speaker – hearer an intricate system of rules that involve mental operations of a very abstract nature, applying to representations that are quite remote from the physical signal.
> – 1968: 52-53

Let us try to understand the implications of the above observations of Chomsky. We can agree that a child can understand a new sentence because of its similarity with some he has learned in the past. But the crucial point is that this similarity is not, in many cases, observable similarity. Suppose we present a child with a sentence he has not heard before, "John was eager to leave". An empiricist or a behaviourist would claim that his understanding of the sentence is due to the observable similarity between it and sentences which he has already learned and understood.

But the point of Chomsky is that it cannot do to say that the child's understanding of "John was eager to leave" is due to his applying to this sentence what he has learned in connection with previously heard and observably similar sentences. For which sentences are they? They will probably include ones like "John was persuaded to leave", and "John was forced to leave" as well as ones like "John was happy to leave". Something, therefore, must explain why the child construes the new sentences as similar in grammar and meaning to sentences of the latter, and not to sentences of the former kind. *Ex-hypothesi*, this cannot be an observable similarity, for that obtains in both cases. Hence, we must postulate that the child is able to identify structural components – the subject and the object of sentences – which are not uniformly correlated with the observable features of utterances.

Evidently, Chomsky does not think that the child's understanding of new sentences can be explained on the basis of observable similarity or inductive generalization. But why he is so sure that the child construes a new sentence in one way rather than another, or can recognize that "John was persuaded to leave", for example, can be paraphrased roughly as "They persuaded John to leave", whereas no such paraphrase is possible in the "eager" case. This can be accounted for if we take into account the importance for Chomsky of our linguistic intuitions. Linguistic intuition, as Chomsky understands it, is the ability to *see* or *judge* about the structural aspects and meanings of sentences. We can judge that sentences are different in spite of apparent similarities between them (*John is eager to please* and *John is easy to please*, to take one example), i.e. we can judge that sentences, though they look alike on the surface, may have different subject–object positions in the deep level. We can see or judge, e.g. that sentences *A* and *B* are more similar in meaning than *A* and *D*. This ensures, according to him, the child's ability to read the new sentence in one way rather than another, or to see that two sentences which look grammatically alike on the surface are really logically different. If this is correct, this clearly proves that the child has knowledge of deep structural components and transformation rules of the language. This also proves, according to Chomsky, that analogy cannot be the criterion for producing and understanding new sentences. The latter ability is due to our knowledge or internal possession of a set of rules and principles that TG grammar proposes to formulate.

Besides, according to Chomsky, there are some empirical considerations which speak in favour of internalized rules and against inductive operations:

i. We find that in a very short time and on the basis of relatively few heard sentences, a child acquires mastery of language. It is difficult to believe that he attains this mastery so speedily solely on the basis of generalization from the small sample he has encountered. This can be explained only with reference to internal possession of rules.

ii. Most of the sentences a child hears around him are ungrammatical, full of errors, distortions and hesitations. If language rules were acquired solely by inductive generalizations, one would expect the child's competence to be infected with the mistakes he has heard. But this does

> not happen. The child may produce many ungrammatical sentences, but the underlying competence to produce the right ones is there. This suggests that the child has internalized a set of rules.

If the foregoing is well taken, a child or a native speaker has mental representation of rules that cannot be taken care of by any inductive generalization. This is the sum and substance of Chomsky's mentalistic account. Evidently, we have taken his mentalism as the thesis of internalized, tacit knowledge of rules, etc. Does this thesis imply that language is subjectively constituted, that it has no being apart from each individual's understanding or knowledge of it? It should be noted that from the fact that speakers have mental representation of rules it does not necessarily follow that language or rules is mental. Yet thinkers like F.D'Agostino (1986) attribute this subjective view to Chomsky. And this is not unreasonable when we remember some of the observations of Chomsky like the following

> ... language, after all, has no existence apart from its mental representation. Whatever properties it has must be those that are given to it by the innate mental processes of the organism that has invented it and that invents it anew with each succeeding generation, along with whatever properties are associated with the conditions of its use. – 1968: 81

> Again, ... it seems that language should be, for this reason, a most illuminating probe with which to explore the organization of mental processes. – Ibid.

Or

> ... in a technical sense, linguistic theory is mentalistic since it is concerned with discovering a mental reality underlying actual behaviour. – Chomsky 1969: 88

We shall however say more about this radical subjectivist thesis in Chapter 4.

But Chomsky's mentalism or his talk about unconscious mental representation of rules, or what he calls competence, does not seem to be complete without being related to the question of innateness. Chomsky has emphatically referred to some unlearned general principles common to all human languages which are programmed into the child's brain as part of his genetic inheritance. Chomsky indeed speaks of the child as being born "with a perfect knowledge of universal grammar, that is, with a fixed schematism that he uses, ... in acquiring language. (1976: 30)"

We must give a brief explanation of linguistic universals which Chomsky divides under: substantive and formal. His accent is, however, more on formal universals (i.e. the general principles that determine the form and mode of operation of the particular languages) than on substantive ones. He observes:

> In general, there is no doubt that a theory of language, regarded as a hypothesis about the innate "language forming capacity" of human, should concern itself with both substantive and formal universals. But whereas substantive universals have been the traditional concern of general linguistic theory, investigation of the abstract conditions that must be satisfied by any generative grammar have been undertaken only quite recently. They seem to offer extremely rich and varied possibilities for study in all aspects of grammar. – 1980: 118

Chomsky talks about a number of formal universals at different times. One of the priniciples is that all languages utilize structure-dependent operation. For example, when interrogatives are formed from indicatives, they are formed not by fortuitous change in word-order, but by the phrase structure out of which the indicatives are derived. Thus, structure-dependent operation takes the following form "permute the whole of the subject noun phrase with the first auxiliary verb, introducing the auxiliary verb *do* for the purpose when there is no other". In this way, we get:

1. Was John present yesterday?
2. Will the man who is honest leave?
3. Is the woman who is winning tired?

from:

1. John was present yesterday.
2. The man who is honest will leave.
3. The woman who is winning is tired.

Another universal principle is what Chomsky calls *A*-over-*A* principle. According to this principle, a transformation rule operates on the larger phrase rather than on a part of it. For example, consider the sentence:

John saw Mary's brother.

According to the *A*-over-*A* principle, the rule that "moves, deletes or otherwise operates upon noun phrases", in the words of Lyons (1990: 102), will apply to the whole noun phrase my brother, and not to a part of it, brother. So we can derive by transformation the sentence:

Mary's brother was seen by John

but not:

Mary was seen brother by John.

The latter sentence will violate *A*-over-*A* constraint.

This constraint applies not only in the context of passive transformation, but in some other contexts as well. For example, let us take the following sentences:

1. For him to understand *this lecture* is difficult.
2. It is difficult for him to understand this lecture.

The underlined parts of these sentences are noun phrases. Now if we apply the rule of interrogative formation to these noun phrases, we get the following corresponding sentences.

1a. What is for him to understand difficult?

2b. What is it difficult for him to understand?

Now note that sentence 1a is ungrammatical, while sentence 2b is grammatical. This can be explained by the *A*-over-*A* principle that 1a violates this rule. For in sentence 1, the noun phrase "this lecture" is contained in another noun phrase, i.e. "for him to understand this lecture"; and the rule of interrogative formation operates only on the noun phrase "this lecture". But in sentence 2, the phrase "for him to understand this lecture" is not a noun phrase, and so the noun phrase "this lecture" is not contained in another noun phrase; accordingly the application of the rule of interrogative formation to the noun phrase "this lecture" in 2a does not violate the *A*-over-*A* principle. There are cases, of course, where the application of this principle involves certain complexity, but we need not consider it.

Another general principle of the transformation rules, according to Chomsky, is that all "non-root transformations" apply cyclically. Chomsky draws a distinction between "root transformation" and "non-root transformation". A transformation rule which does not apply to embedded sentences, but to the full sentence structure is called "root transformation". The rule for constructing "yes/no" question is a "root transformational" rule: for example, the interrogative derived from the sentence "The man who is acquainted with me was here", would be "Was the man who is acquainted with me here?" But in the case of non-root transformation the rule applies to the embedded structure of a sentence. Thus, from the initial phrase structure "I wonder John is visiting *WH*- someone" we can derive the sentence "I wonder who John is visiting", and not "I wonder who is John visiting". Now, Chomsky observes that in the cases where a sentence contains more than one cyclic category (i.e. the category which can serve as the domain of transformation), the non-root transformation first applies to that category which does not contain any other cyclic category, next it applies to that category which immediately contains this one and so on. This is what Chomsky means when he says transformational rules operate cyclically. Among other cases, this principle of cyclic application explains why from the following sentence 1a we can deduce 1b, but not 1e by pronominalization.

1a. Smith was informed that Smith had won.

1b. Smith was informed that he had won.

1c. He was informed that Smith had won.

In Chomsky's opinion, the fact that 1c cannot be derived from 1a can be explained if we assume that pronominalization applies cyclically. Note that the underlying structure of 1a has an embedded constituent "that Smith had won". According to the principle of cyclic application, pronominalization should operate finally on this constituent, and this is precisely what has been done in 1b. But the derivation of 1c violates the principle of cyclic application, thus it is not allowed. Here type facts like this one.

Facts like this one, according to Chomsky, motivate the introduction of the principle of cyclic application in the universal grammar.

We would mention two more principles admitted in Chomskyan theory of universal grammar which imposes restriction on the operation of transformational rules. One of these two is the condition of subjacency. According to this condition, if a cyclic category *B* contains another category *A*, and is itself contained in yet another category *C*, then transformation should not move an item within the category *A* to a position in the domain of *C*. Thus, from the underlying structure:

(a) (NP (NP the one that I like) of Tolstoy's novels) is out of print to derive (b) would be wrong; and

(b) (NP (NP the only one) of Tolstoy's novels) is out of print that I like.

It can be shown that (b) has been derived from (a) by

violating the subjacency condition. The phrase "that I like" is an element of a noun phrase which is contained in another noun phrase, while the latter is itself contained in another domian (let us call it C). In (b) we find that the phrase "that I like" has been moved to the domain C, and thus it violates subjacency.

In Chomsky's opinion, the principle of subjacency is an important generalization. He analyses a number of transformational rules like "NP-preposition", and "WH movement" to demonstrate that all these rules are governed by the subjacency condition.

Chomsky holds that "specified-subject condition" is yet another restriction on the application of transformational rules. This constraint prevents both the elimination of an element from an embedded phrase and also its association with an element outside of this phrase if

(i) the embedded phrase is either a sentence or a noun phrase, and

(ii) the embedded phrase contains a subject which is distinct from the element under consideration.

This restriction explains why the following sentence 1a is not well-formed, although 1b is well-formed:

1a. We expected John to like each other.

1b. Each of us expected John to like the other.

It is to be noted that 1a has an embedded clause "John to like each other". To be well-formed the phrase "each other" must have to be related to the expression "We" ("us"). But the specified subject condition forbids this relation because the embedded phrase "John to like each other" contains a subject "John" which is distinct from "each other".

These universal principles governing the form of grammatical rules in particular languages, Chomsky explicitly points out, restrict or dictate the hypotheses that the child formulates on the basis of scanty data of the language to which he is exposed and that ultimately acquires mastery of it. In other words, when a child hears the utterances of the language he is to master, he is able to formulate many hypotheses about how sentences are to be produced, interpreted, formed and transformed some of which are compatible with the facts about the language he is to master. In this way, he internalizes the rules of his particular language and becomes a fluent speaker of it. The position of the child is analogous to that of a scientist. He equally approaches the data like the scientist with a set of hypotheses and tries to find which among these hypotheses will fit the observed data and his linguistic intuitions. The only difference is that in the case of a child the highly restrictive general principles that are a part of his mind determine or put a constraint on what hypotheses he can formulate and ultimately lead to his internalization of the rules of a particular language. Therefore, in Chomsky's thesis there is a profound connection between competence and innateness in the sense of unlearned regulative principles which have a definite say in our internalization of rules.

# 2

# Chomsky on the Relation between Competence, Performance and Creativity

In this chapter, we shall try to understand the following aspects of Chomsky's position: 1. Chomsky's account of competence as distinct from performance; and 2. his claim that it is in terms of competence that one can produce and understand indefinite number of sentences, that language can be "creative".

1. Chomsky makes a distinction between competence (the speaker–hearer's knowledge of his language) and performance (the actual use of language in concrete situations). Knowledge of language, according to Chomsky, is really the knowledge of rules and principles governing sentence-connection and interpretation. When people have this knowledge or competence, they can judge whether a sentence is grammatical or whether it follows the rules of sentence construction and interpretation.

But this use of the concept of competence seems different from the usual one which is emphasized particularly by Gilbert Ryle in his *The Concept of Mind* (1980). Competence in the usual sense is an ability. As Ryle puts it, it "is not the knowledge, or ignorance, of this or that truth, but the ability, or inability, to do certain sorts of things" (1980: 28). Thus when in ordinary life we talk about competence, we are interested more in "what it is for someone to know how to perform task" than in "cognitive repertoires" (ibid.). This is to prevent the Cartesian myth that any activity should be steered by a prior mental operation occurring in the "ghost in the machine". Ryle's point is that what is involved in our competence "to make and appreciate jokes, to talk grammatically, to play chess, to fish or to argue" is not any antecedent mental monologue, but simply the fact that we can "perform them well, i.e. correctly or efficiently or successfully" (ibid.: 29). To put the contention of Ryle in a more straightforward way, his account of competence as a kind of ability agrees more with our commonsense intuition than Chomsky's account of competence does. Of course, Ryle speaks of many kinds of ability like "capacity", "tendency" or "propensity" (ibid.: 119). But for our purpose, it is enough to say that any talk about a person's competence amounts to what he can do. Now any statement about what one can do is conditional in form, i.e. it is a statement about what one would do if certain conditions are fulfilled. Thus, "John can be a champion in a chess competition" if he does some such things like these:

- If he is careful about his moves with the pawns.
- If he practises seriously.
- If he prevents his opponent from making moves that will go against him.

Similarly, "John is able to understand French" if he does some such things like these:

- If he learns French.
- If he is addressed in French, or shown any French newspaper, he responds appropriately.
- If he translates French sentences into his mother tongue.

It follows from the foregoing that, when we talk about a person's competence, we should concentrate not on what is going on within his head or mind, but on performance, not on what he *knows* but on what he *does*. Of course, there is a sense of "know" which can be equivalent to competence. "Know" in this sense will be "know how" which will be conditional in form and will not be "know" in the categorized sense. A man is said to know how to play if, in the words of Ryle,

> he normally does make the permitted moves, avoid the forbidden moves and protest if his opponent makes for bidden moves. His knowledge how is exercised primarily in the moves that he makes, or concedes, and in the moves that he avoids or vetoes. – 1980: 41

It goes without saying that when Chomsky equates "competence" with "know", he has in view not "know how" but "know" of a more serious kind. For competence, according to him, is a case of mental representation of rules which Ryle would identify as knowing that. But as already stated before, Chomsky's use of the term "competence" is against our common sense. We normally take "competence" as "ability" or "know how" and accordingly we think, unlike Chomsky, that since competence is conditional, it cannot be identical with what we categorically know which, strictly speaking, does not admit of any condition.

Similarly, Hymes points out that it is out of keeping with that usual concept of "competence" if "competence is knowledge of sentences only as grammatical" in Chomsky's wide sense of "grammatical", and not "competence as to when to speak, when not, and as to what to talk about with whom, when, where, in what manner" – competence, as he rightly observes, that is "fed by social experience, needs and motives" (Hymes 1979: 277-78). Of course, we doubt whether the point of Ryle or Hymes as it stands would worry Chomsky much. He may yet respond with unruffled conviction that what he means by "competence" is only knowledge or mental representation of rules. May be his choice of the word is unadvisable, but that will not affect his substantial position.

Thus Chomsky's knowledge of language is not the ability to use it on the appropriate occasion. As Chomsky observes:

> ... the question of what constitutes knowledge of language and how this knowledge is used are often assimilated. Thus, it is often held that to speak and understand a language is to have a practical ability, rather like the ability to ride a bicycle or play chess. More generally, to have knowledge, in this view, is to have certain abilities and skills. ... But the idea that knowledge is ability is entirely untenable. Simple considerations show that this conception can hardly be correct.
>
> Consider two people who share exactly the same knowledge of Spanish. Their pronunciation, knowledge of the meaning of words, grasp of sentence structure, and so on, are identical. Nevertheless, these two people may – and characteristically – do differ greatly in their ability to use the language. – 1988: 9

Since linguistic knowledge is unconnected with conditions of actual use, in our account of competence we should disregard all reference to appropriateness to the situation, and to the social and communication factors usually connected with "use" of language.

As Chomsky puts it:

> In ordinary usage ... when we speak of a language, we have in mind some kind of social phenomenon, a shared property of a community. What kind of community? There is no clear answer to this question. – Ibid.: 37

Or:

> Putnam's statement that *"Languages and meanings are cultural realities"* (his emphasis) is accurate in one sense. ... But these "cultural realities" do not contribute to understanding how language is acquired, understood and used, ... how it is related to other faculties of mind. ............ –Chomsky 1995: 50-51

Again:

> Language is used for expression of thought ... with no particular concern for commumcation. – 1988: 38

Hence in our description of "competence" we should rather confine our attention to a-social rules and principles which are mentally represented and which contribute to the well-formedness of sentences, and the structural and semantic descriptions assigned to them.

From the foregoing it follows that Chomsky confines lingustic knowledge to something abstracted from actual use in context or as Strawson puts it, from "communication intention".

This does not, however, mean that Chomsky recognizes no relation between competence and performance or use. In fact, he insists that competence, in his sense, partly explains our actual linguistic behaviour. As he puts it, "Rules form mental representations, which enter into our speaking ..." (Chomsky 1990: 641). Or:

> This was a significant shift of point of view: from behaviour and its products to the system of knowledge represented in the mind/brain that underlies behaviour. – Ibid.

Chomsky's point is effectively put forward by Devitt and Sterelny (1987: 132). Just as "what makes acertain movement of a ball, a good tennis shot" can be explained by properties like "speed, direction and height" in the physical world outside, analogously what promotes a certain behaviour such as producing a good or appropriate sentence, or understanding it well can be explained by an account of competence as something psychological or mentally represented. To be more explicit and precise, a skilful performer is one with

(a) Chomskyan knowledge of language (competence), and

(b) what Chomsky would regard as non-linguistic knowledge (e.g. of the appropriateness of using one way of speaking rather than another in this or that situation).

For example, to speak English well (performance) one requires:

(i) knowledge of English language, and

(ii) knowledge how and in what manner to speak to other fellow beings, how to use sentences relevantly in a particular situation.

In this way (a) knowledge of language together with (b) knowledge of relevance or appropriateness will explain performance.

It follows that Chomsky makes a distinction between (a) and (b). This is revealed explicitly when, e.g. *in* Rules and Representations he distinguishes between "grammatical competence" and "pragmatic competence". He says: By "grammatical competence" I mean the cognitive state that encompasses all these aspects of form and meaning and their relation, which are properly assigned to the specific sub-system of the human mind that relates representations of form and meaning.

"Pragmatic competence", he holds, "underlies the ability to use such knowledge along with the conceptual system to achieve certain ends or purposes" (1980a: 59). But if we learn from Wittgenstein, we may raise the question of whether such a distinction between "know" and "know-how", between grammatical and pragmatic competence is not an artificial one. For, in a very plausible sense, the notion of knowledge or understanding is identical with the notion of a capacity to do something, with know-how. To understand a language means to have an ability, to be master of a technique, to possess a practical skill. Since understanding (or knowledge) is essentially connected with use or with the capacity to do certain things with signs, there is no gap between knowledge or understanding and use, as Chomsky would suppose. Rather, the operations of understanding consist in what one overtly does. If this analysis is correct, Chomsky's distinction between knowledge of language and non-linguistic knowledge is not beyond doubt.

Again, if we follow Ryle, we do not think it is part of the everyday notion of competence that competence is something that explains performance. To say that I manage to ride my bicycle to work each day without falling off because I am a competent bicyclist sounds a rather empty explanation. We shall see now two other relations between competence and performance emerge when Chomsky tries to show how competence explains creativity.

2. So we come to the contention of Chomsky that competence can explain the creativity of language. But, here, we encounter some shifts and uncertainties in Chomsky, and correspondingly shifts in the relation between competence and performance.

a. First he shows the interconnection between competence and creativity in the following way:

> The central fact to which any significant linguistic theory must address itself is this: a mature speaker can produce a new sentence of his language on the appropriate occasion, and other speakers can understand it immediately, though it is equally new to them. ... Normal mastery of a language involves ... the ability to understand immediately an indefinite number of entirely new sentences. ... (I)t is clear that a theory of language that neglects this "creative" aspect of language is of only marginal interest.
>
> – Chomksy 1964: 51

From the above passage, it appears that normal mastery of language, which can be safely equated with competence, involves the ability to understand new sentences not encountered before. Of course, in the above passage, Chomsky talks about a mature speaker who can produce a new sentence of his language on the appropriate occasion. But this reference to "appropriate occasion" should not make us think that creativity is an aspect of performance. But when we come to the end of the paper, "Current Issues in Linguistic Theory" from which we have taken the above observation of Chomsky, we find that Chomsky rebukes modern linguistics for having "failed totally to come to grips with the 'creative' aspect of language use, that is the ability to form and understand previously unheard sentences". Thus Chomsky talks about creative aspect of language use, and is not language use a matter of performance? Therefore, should we say that a recursive set of rules embodies the speaker's competence and the creative aspect of language use is a matter of performance? But we need not have this kind of worry. As is evident, the creative aspect of language use is described by Chomsky as the ability to form and understand previously unheard sentences and it is the sameability that Chomsky also describes as the creative aspect of language. Hence, the creative aspect of language and the creative aspect of language use have been taken in the same way as the ability to produce and comprehend new sentences. It is said that transformational grammar represents the competence that involves this ability.

In sum, Chomsky's mention of "the creative aspect of language use" should not be taken very seriously. For, his real intention is to underline that performance on the appropriate occasion, in his own words, is "not the focus of inquiry"; it is rather "one source of evidence for the internal systems of the mind/brain. ..." (Chomsky 1990: 641).

Thus follows another relation between competence and performance. Competence or creativity is not an aspect of performance; linguistic behaviour or performance, on the contrary, it is merely evidence of competence or creative capacity. It should be noted in this connection that Chomsky makes it a point to deny that linguistic behaviour provides us with a criterion. As he observes:

> One might attempt to characterize knowledge of language, as a capacity or ability to do something, as a system of dispositions of some kind, in which case one might be led (misled, I think) to conclude that behaviour provides a criterion for the possession of knowledge. – 1980a: 48

We may pursue this point of evidence vs criterion a bit. A criterion for something, as distinct from an evidence, is a mark the presence or absence of which indicates respectively the presence or absence of the thing in question. But in the case of an evidence though the presence of the mark (which is the evidence) counts as an indication of the presence of the thing for which it is an evidence, its absence will not signify the absence of the thing. Hence, Chomsky by his emphasis on evidence means that a person cannot be said to be lacking in knowledge of language or competence if and when he fails to exhibit successful performances. Indeed, a native speaker is considered to be a competent speaker even when he frequently fails to use and understand certain sentences appropriately, and his failure is generally explained in terms of some non-linguistic factors. This is no doubt a good point. The claim that successful linguistic performance is a mark of the possession of the knowledge of language, while any deviation from it is a sign that one lacks the knowledge seems to be untenable simply because it confines linguistic knowledge to ideal speakers, leaving aside all native speakers.

Chomsky offers a few more arguments to establish that the capacity to use language is only evidence for the possession of the linguistic competence. For example, he argues, as already said before, that it is quite conceivable that two individuals have the same amount of knowledge of language although they differ in their ability to express that knowledge in practice. In other words, despite possessing the same knowledge two individuals may vary in their capacity to use that knowledge. Thus from the fact that one lacks the capacity to use language correctly on some occasions, it would be unfair to conclude that one does not possess the required knowledge. Hence, performance is only an evidence of competence, and by no means its criterion.

b. There are, however, passages in Chomsky where there is a shift when in discussing the creative aspect of language use, there is a stronger emphasis on appropriateness to the situation. Thus, in *Language and Mind* we find the following passage:

> When we study human language, we are approaching what some might call the human essence, the distinctive qualities of mind that are, so far as we know, unique to man and that are inseparable from any critical phase of human existence, personal or social. Hence the fascination of this study, and, no less its frustration. The frustration arises from the fact that despite much progress, we remain as incapable as before of coming to grips with the core problem of human language, which I take to be this: Having mastered a language, one is able to understand an indefinite number of expressions that are new to one's experience, that bear no simple physical resemblance and are in no simple way analogous to the expressions that constitute one's linguistic experience; *and one is able, with greater or less facility, to produce such expresstions on an appropriate occasion* (emphasis mine), despite their novelty and independently of detectable stimulus configurations,

> and to be understood by others who share this still mysterious ability. The normal use of language is, in this sense, a creative activity. This creative aspect of normal language use is one fundamental factor that distinguishes human language from any known system of human communication. – 1972: 100

Again, in *Language and Problems of Knowledge*, he continues in the same way:

> Let us return to Descartes's problem, the problem of how language is used in the normal creative fashion. ... (W)hat I have in mind is something more mundane: the ordinary use of language in everyday life, with its distinctive properties of novelty, freedom from control by external stimuli and inner states, coherence and appropriateness to situations, and its capacity to evoke appropriate thoughts in the listener. – 1988: 138

The above passages reveal that Chomsky does not hesitate to emphasize the role of appropriate occasion in producing sentences, and this seems to tie the creative aspect of language use with appropriate performance. Previously, competence involved the ability to produce and understand new sentences, and so competence was interlinked with creativity. But now a different picture seems to be suggested. Creativity or the ability to produce and understand different sentences is more closely related to language behaviour or use, to the coherence and appropriateness of ordinary speech, and to normal situated use of language. Now if creativity is to be connected with competence, the position will be something like this. Since an important aspect of creative behaviour is its coherence and appropriateness to the situation, it should be the ability or competence to use language coherently and appropriately. But unfortunately this is what Chomsky's standard account of competence as internalization of these cursive rules of grammar will not allow.

What is most crucial, the shift results in the kind of relation between competence and performance that Chomsky generally rejects. Chomsky's usual position is this: skilful, appropriate, etc. performance is simply empirical evidence for linguistic competence (rather as spots are the evidence of measles). But in some of the passages we mention, where more emphasis is put on actual use, it can begin to look as if, for Chomsky, competence is connected with the ability to use language appropriately and coherently. This will mean that performance is a criterion for competence: i.e. that part of our very understanding of competence is in terms of performance (rather as, according to Wittgenstein, certain sorts of behaviour are criteria for pain-part of our very understanding of the concept of pain). Chomsky's own position, surely, is that, despite the passages where he emphasizes performance, performance remains at most empirical evidence for linguistic competence and other kinds of knowledge. Still, the very fact that he feels compelled to refer to performance might be a sign that the connection between competence and performance is tighter, more "criteria", than he officially allows.

## II

It is not obvious, however, that this should be regarded as a substantial criticism of Chomsky; perhaps it simply shows that he sometimes expresses himself loosely when he attempts to define creativity, competence, etc. and that despite some shifts and uncertainties in his way of speaking, he continues to confine linguistic knowledge to something divorced from actual use in context, etc. His position will then remain that the semantic and syntactical rules mastery of which is knowledge of language or competence is not really rules for "communicating" at all.

It is perfectly possible for someone to have a perfect linguistic competence without bothering himself about "communication".

But if this is the contention that Chomsky intends to insist on, we may respond to it in the following way.

It is doubtful whether we can free the notion of competence from all essential connection with communication intention. Chomsky, of course, would not eulogize the social aspect of language by describing communication as the essential or primary function of language. He would insist that when a speaker uses language, his intention may be to amuse the audience, to keep the conversation going, to lest his voice and several other things. It is true, no doubt, that we can do various things with language. But how does it go against the primacy of the communicative use of language, unless Chomsky shows what he exactly means by "primary", why the communicative use of language is not primary or why he can refuse communication to be the primary function of language when this is at odds with our common sense as well as with quite a long and respectable philosophic tradition. Is there not the danger that his disinclination comes only as a package deal with the specific theory that he proposes? All these require serious arguments which we miss in Chomsky.

Our contention is strengthened more by Strawson's emphasis on "communication intention", particularly in his paper "Meaning and Truth" (2012: 91-102). Let us follow him faithfully. According to him, we generally, and quite reasonably, think of linguistic meaning in terms of and semantic rules and conventions. Since "rules or conventions govern human practices and purposive human activities", we should enquire, "what purposive activities are governed by these conventions. What are these rules as rules for doing?" The answer is, as he emphatically points out, these rules are, precisely, rules for communicating, rules by following which our communication – intention is fulfilled. In other words, "it is not just a fortunate fact" that these rules are used for this communicative purpose, rather it is the very nature of the rules that "they are seen as rules where by this purpose can be achieved" (Strawson 2012: 92).

Thus, it will not be finally feasible to separate competence or knowledge of language from communication intention. For example, we cannot really divorce what it is to understand the categories of subject and object from aspects of communication and intention (such as what we primarily intend to talk about in a conversation). We use an active sentence, "John opens the door", thus emphasizing the subject "John" when we intend to communicate something about the doer of an action. But if we intend to communicate exactly what has been done to the object "window", how it is affected by John's activity, we use the passive sentence, "The window is opened by John". All such things reveal that linguistic structures and categories are always interwoven with different communicative purposes.

The above response may not satisfy Chomsky. It may seem to him a little hard to swallow. Is it not possible, he would argue, to drop any reference to communication intention, and instead entertain a reference to, say, belief expression? This may sound plausible, since, in the words of Strawson, "we of temvoice our thoughts to ourselves with no communicative intention" (2012: 98). This is exactly the point that Chomsky insists on when he holds:

> As a graduate student I spent two years writing a lengthy manuscript, assuming throughout that it will never be published or read by anyone. I meant everything I wrote, intending nothing as to what anyone would believe about my beliefs, in fact taking it for granted that there would be no audience.
> – 1976: 61

In reply to this, we must appreciate, with Strawson, that "there is nothing in the concept of a language to rule out the idea that every individual might have his own language which only he understands". But at the same time, it is an agreed point, as Strawson rightly points out, that "language is public", "that linguistic rules are more or less socially common rules" and "that the possession of a public language enlarges the mind" by bringing us into relation with others, "that there are beliefs one could not express without a language to express them in, thoughts one could not entertain without a rule-governed system of expressions for articulating them" (2012: 100).

And people acquire mastery of such a system of language for expressing and communicating their beliefs through training as children by the elder members of a community. "If this is the way the game has to be played", as P.F. Straws on puts it, "then the communication theorist must be allowed to have won it" (ibid.: 101).

# 3

# Chomsky on the Native Speaker's Knowledge of Language

In this chapter, we shall do two things: (i) First we shall give a very brief account of Chomsky's account of unconscious or tacit knowledge, and (ii) second, we shall critically examine his position.

(i) We can safely claim that a linguist has knowledge about a language. "What is knowledge of language?" Answer: "Language is a computational system, a rule system of some sort. Knowledge of language is knowledge of this rule system" (Chomsky 1990: 641). Hence, to say that a linguist has knowledge about language is to say that he knows that it is described by certain rules and principles. But the problem is "Can we make the same claim about native speakers too?" To this, Chomsky's response will be affirmative, only with the qualification that the linguistic knowledge of the native speakers is unconscious.

The point of Chomsky is that a native speaker has knowledge of language, though it is not possible for him to spell out linguistic rules like a professional linguist. He cannot really acknowledge what the rules, etc. of language are, that rules, etc. of his language are so-and-so. So Chomsky introduces *unconscious knowledge* of the rules and principles of language in order to describe the competence of a native speaker. In other words, the contention of Chomsky is that we should attribute to speakers the knowledge the linguist has it is just that ordinary or native speakers only possess this knowledge unconsciously.

(ii) But the question is whether it is really possible for a native speaker to know the rules, etc. of language although he cannot articulate them. In fact, what will be the nature of unconscious knowledge? Can we really call it knowledge in spite of its evident dissimilarities to more standard cases of knowledge? It will be useful in this connection to make clear certain plausible assumptions about knowledge which we often make. These assumptions are:

a. Knowledge must be avowable.

b. Someone who knows *X* must know that he knows *X*.

c. Someone who knows *X* must be able to justfy his claim that *X*.

d. Knowledge that *X* must intelligibly link up with other items of knowledge, i.e. one would hesitate to ascribe knowledge that *X* to someone if he also asserted things which are clearly incompatible with *X*.

These assumptions, while indeed plausible, have of course been challenged by various philosophers. Their challenges, typically, have taken the form of relaxing or weakening the criteria for knowledge contained in the assumptions. It would, then, be premature to reject Chomsky's account of knowledge of language on the ground that it violates one or more of the assumptions so far stated. In what follows, therefore, we shall be considering not only whether that account violates the assumptions as stated above, but also whether it is compatible with more relaxed, weaker versions of them. We shall argue that Chomsky's account violates the constraints on knowledge imposed by even those weaker versions, in which case, on any tolerable characterization of knowledge, it is not knowledge of which Chomsky is speaking.

Let us begin with Michael Devitt and Kim Sterelny who make the following observation on the thesis of tacit knowledge:

> ... the transformational grammarians usually write as if they had a surprising view of how the grammar is built into speakers: the speakers are alleged to know "tacitly" the rules of a grammar. We think that this view is quite mistaken.
>
> – 1987: 134

Thus the contention of Devitt and Sterelny is that it will be wrong to attribute knowledge to native speakers. To explain this, let us attend to what is involved in following a rule. Let us suppose that *R* is a rule for addition. Now about an adder we can say any of the following things:

(a) He behaves as if he follows *R*.

(b) He actually follows *R*.

(c) He knows that *R* is an algorithm and applies it.

Let us explain in some details the distinctions between the three senses we have just drawn above (b), i.e. "actually following a rule" indeed differs from (a), i.e. behaving as if one is following it. Suppose a boy knows only how to write digits but does not know the rule of addition. Now if he just copies from a book of arithmetic that the sum of 68 and 57 is 125, then he is behaving as if he is following a rule. It is only a case of "behaving" since if queried, the boy will not be able to answer why the sum of 68 and 57 is 125. But this is not the case with "actually following a rule *R*". In order for someone (or something) to be actually following a rule and not just behaving as if it were, reference to the rule must play a genuine role in explaining the behaviour. In the case of a person, for example, he must be able to recognize mistakes, even if he cannot spell out the rule which, when he makes a mistake, he is violating. In the case of a machine, the rules play an explanatory role in virtue of the programmer's having installed them and the fact that we can speak of the machine having gone wrong if it does certain things. So in (a) *R* has no explanatory or causal value while indeed it has in (b). But the most crucial thing that the grammarian's theory of competence will need is that we follow rules in sense (iii), i.e. our actual rule following must presuppose our knowledge of rule. This, according to Devitt and Sterelny, is an impossibility. If, for example, *R* is built into a machine, say a pocket calculator, then it is true that it actually follows *R*. If *R* is not built into a calculator, then also it may behave as if it follows *R*. But the most important point is that no kind of prior knowledge is necessary for applying *R*. It is not true that one cannot actually follow *R* without knowing that *R* is an algorithm for addition. As a matter of fact, a calculator can follow *R* without knowing that *R* is an algorithm for addition. Strictly speaking, to speak of knowledge in the case of a machine makes no sense. In the words of Devitt and Sterelny:

> Consider ... the pocket calculator. Suppose, it is built to follow *R*. ... We sense a strain in ascribing any sort of knowledge to a calculator. ... What we are insisting on is that it does not have propositional knowledge of *R*. ... We can be certain that the calculator does not have it. ... – Ibid.: 136

This denial of knowledge, as they further point out, requires some clarification, since "know" is ordinarily used both loosely and in a variety of contexts, such as:

(a) John knows David.

(b) John knows who little Mary is.

(c) John knows how to add.

(d) John knows rule *R* for addition.

(e) John knows that *R* is an algorithm for addition.

We are however interested in the last three, i.e. knowing-how, knowing-a-rule and knowing-that. Knowing-how is a matter of having certain practical abilities or skills. Knowing-that is cognitive and involves mental representation or propositional knowledge. In the case of knowing-how, however, e.g. knowing-how to swim or ride a bicycle, no mental representation is necessary. We just ride a bicycle, and that's all.

It appears that Chomsky's knowledge of language is not a case of knowing-how. If knowledge of language is not a case of knowing-how, then is it a case of knowing-that which (d) and (c) seem to presuppose?

In reply to this, Harman points out that the native speaker's knowledge of language which Chomsky speaks of is unmistakably a case of knowing-that. As he puts it:

> He (Chomsky) also takes a grammar to describe competence as the knowledge that the language is described by the rules of the grammar. – Harman 1971: 379

But Chomsky strongly reacts against Harman for attributing such a view to him:

> Obviously it is absurd to suppose that the speaker of the language knows the rules in the sense of being able to state them. – Hook 1969: 86[1]

In spite of the above protest of Chomsky, we have the suspicion that Chomsky has indulged in knowing-that on several occasions. D.E. Cooper notes one such occasion when he observes:

> Suffice it to say that we find mentalism in action when Chomsky explains a person's ability to recognize that "In has lived Mary Princeton" is not a proper interrogative form by his "knowing-that" a certain structure-dependent operation has not been performed in deriving it. – 1975: 24

Chomsky's knowledge of language, then, is knowledge *that* Stephen Stich articulates the following difficulty in this position

---

[1] In this book there is interesting dialogue between Chomsky and Harman.

(Devitt and Sterelny 1987: 138). If a person knows that *P* or that these are the rules, etc. of language, it is expected that he is either aware of them or would be aware of them under a suitable prompt. But the native speaker has not this awareness. He cannot avow them; he does not know that he knows them, nor can he justify them. So we cannot claim that he knows that ... in the paradigmatic sense. One most important criterion of knowing that in the paradigmatic or standard sense will be this. If a person knows that *P* it will link up with his other beliefs. For example, if he knows that this is a cat, it is linked up with his other beliefs that it is a small, furry four-legged *animal*, that it mews and does not bark, etc. But this is not the way a native speaker knows. It is only after some training that the native speaker can understand even the relatively simple claim that *NP* → Det + Adj + N is a rule of English. Since he has no background and is not aware of what the rules of English are, we cannot say that the simple rule of English he has just learned is integrated with his other beliefs about rules of English which he evidently does not possess. Consequently, he cannot be said to have (propositional) knowledge of language.

In the foregoing, we have tried to pinpoint that Chomsky's alleged knowledge of language does not satisfy one or other of our standard assumptions about knowledge. Does it mean that we should give up so quickly the task of defending Chomsky's claim that the native speakers have knowledge of language? Should we not at least try to look for some alternative account of knowledge to the one usually assumed? Indeed, there is some plausibility of that if we follow the line of argument that Cooper has described following a clue from Fodor (Cooper 1975: 62). This argument puts the accent on the "aetiology of behaviour", where knowledge is identified typically on the basis of the behaviour it produces. According to this understanding of knowledge, both *A* and *B* have knowledge that *P* if they are in the same states. They will be in the same states if the behaviours they exhibit are equivalent. In other words, *A*, who knows or avows or is aware that *P*, behaves in a particular way *X*; if *B* behaves in the way *X*, he will be in the same state as *A* and knows that *P* even though he is not aware that *P*. Thus, behavioural equivalence decides whether we know that *P*, no matter whether we are conscious or unconscious about it. This is exactly the point of unconscious knowledge which Chomsky attributes to native speakers. A native speaker may be unconscious or unaware of the rules, etc. of knowledge, yet he knows them in the significant sense of the term if his behaviour is relevantly similar to the behaviour of the one who avows that he knows *P*. For he is then in a functionally equivalent state to the second person.

From the foregoing, we find an important and familiar argument for holding that ordinary speakers possess knowledge of language even if they cannot articulate it like a professional linguist. If we approve of the spirit of this argument, it will yield the following conclusion. Awareness and avowability are not at all indispensable for knowing or believing that *p* as we usually assume. All that is needed are equivalent patterns of behaviour which will settle whether we know (irrespective of our being conscious or unconscious of what is allegedly known). It is relevant to point out that "behaviour", in the present context, will include the expression of those "linguistic intuitions" Chomsky talks about, e.g. that two very different sentences are nevertheless very close. In meaning, or that a certain sentence is ambiguous (e.g. Flying planes, in be dangerous), or that certain strings of word are not grammatically acceptable. Since the native speakers have such relevant linguistic intuitions can exhibit them just like the informed linguistics, they also have the relevant knowledge or beliefs.

Hence emerges a seemingly promising line of argument in Chomsky's favour. But is it really so? First of all, we know that there are explicit differences in the response patterns between the two persons – the one who *un-controversially* knows that *p* and the one who *unconsciously* knows that *p*. If I know uncontroversially that David takes his class on Kant every Wednesday, I shall definitely protest or do something like that if my friend denies it. Perhaps this will not be the reaction pattern I know it unconsciously. So we must have to find out whether there is any common link between the behaviour exhibited by the two people one conscious and another unconscious in virtue of which we can identify them as being in the same states. That is surely a very difficult task. Suppose we can overcome that, we shall still be under another difficulty. What do we really mean when we say that I know that *p*, for example that the sun is up in the sky? As already noted, a reasonable assumption is that when a person knows that *p*, he recognizes that he knows that *p*. Now on the proposed understanding of knowledge in terms of states apt to cause behaviour, it seems that recognition of one's knowledge must consist in recognition that one is in a state apt for producing certain behaviour. But this is surely an implausible view. It is neither necessary nor sufficient for recognizing that one knows something that one should recognize one's being in such a state ... etc. ... This is not the standard way we think of knowledge. Hence we doubt whether identification of knowledge in terms of states apt to produce behaviour is possible. If this is not possible, Chomsky's case does not seem to be persuasive.

Again, that behaviour cannot warrant ascription of an internal state of knowledge is also suggested by adopting a powerful consideration of Quines. Quine's position is an important one, which needs spelling out in some detail. He argues that attributions of meaning to the minds of speakers, which go beyond the behavioural evidence, are necessarily indeterminate and for that reason should not be made. To explain this, let us consider his famous "Gavagai" example. Suppose on seeing a rabbit running past a native shouts, "Gavagai". Now an English translator may try different translation manuals in order to translate this in various ways – either as "rabbit" or as "a part of a rabbit" or as "a stage in the life history of a rabbit". Whatever way he translates, the translation will be appropriate to the stimulus-condition of the native's utterance. So the evidence of the stimulus-conditions cannot decide which of the translations is the correct one.

We can now utilize this "indeterminacy" argument against the proposed argument in Chomsky's way as sketched just above. If the speaker's linguistic behaviour is compatible with many different rules, we should not – in the absence of further argument – attribute to him knowledge of any one of these. Let us explain this point a little by starting from the following observation of Stich: "Grammar is afflicted with an embarrassment of riches" (Stich 1972: 807). This means that there can be many alternative but extensionally equivalent "sets of rules, structures or categories" for the generation of the same sentences of a language. Now behavioural consequences will not register my dillerencc if the two speakers "know" different sets of rules or structures. Behavioural evidence, i.e. generation or production of sentences, is all that we have at our disposal and it cannot decide what particular beliefs or knowledge speakers have. Hence, according to the condition of Quine, we cannot attribute any knowledge or belief to a person, because we have no way of telling what he believes.

We have been trying to review the plausibility of an alternative understanding of knowledge in the light of the "aetiology of behaviour" in order to support Chomsky's proposed knowledge of language. So far the outcome is not hopeful.

Another way to defend Chomsky's position may be that ordinary speakers need not be able to justify the rules which allegedly they know. According to this position, ordinary speakers have indeed unreflecting beliefs or knowledge about their language although they cannot justify it. For example, they know that "bachelor" and "unmarried man" have the same meaning or that regular nouns have "S" in the plural, etc. These beliefs are so obvious and self-evident that they entertain and know them without any kind of external confirmation or justification. These are the things that they know simply by participating in a particular speaking community. Or, the natural and unreflective beliefs that the native speakers have about their language result in their being, in the words of Cooper, "trained in and engaged in certain practices as part of their social life" (1975: 82). It is only the native speakers as participants in a practice who can be said to know even though they cannot justify it. Arguably, Wittgenstein and Merleau-Ponty have made the same point.

Wittgenstein in *Philosophical Investigations* emphasizes that language belongs to a form of life. In a similar way, Merleau-Ponty quotes Wittgenstein with approval:

> ... language ... is a manifestation, a revelation of intimate being and of the psychic link which unites us to the world and our follow men. – 1967: 196

Again:

> When I speak or when I understand, I experience the presence of other in myself and of myself in others, a presence which is the cornerstone of inter subjectivity. ... – 1982: 571

Therefore, according to Wittgenstein and Merleau-Ponty, a common form of life is interwoven with language. They seem to in site on the point that peoples' agreement about judgement regarding rules of language is the consequence of their participation or of their being trained within a common form of life. Often these people do not or cannot justify why they apply the rules they do; yet we cannot say that they do not know.

Now the fundamental question that concerns us is, whether this account of unjustifiable knowledge as given by Wittgenstein and Merleau-Ponty will help Chomsky's cause. Our answer will be negative. Even if we concede that there can be knowledge of language by speakers which they cannot justify, this will not help Chomsky. For the knowledge ordinary speakers cannot justify is the kind which they are bound to have simply as participants in a language. In other words, although the speakers cannot justify their knowledge of, e.g. that "bachelor" means the same as "unmarried man" by appealing to semantic rules, or whatever, they can nevertheless justify it in a sense, simply by appealing to their being participants in the language, that is, "I know this because I am a native English speaker" can, in such cases, constitute a justification of what one claims to know. But this alternative cannot do much for Chomsky. One cannot justify an obviously theoretical, and perhaps very complicated, item of alleged knowledge by simply saying, "Because I belong to the community in which that sort of thing is part of participant understanding".

To sum up, I have stated very briefly Chomsky's contention that native speakers have knowledge of language or knowledge of the "rule system". Then I have considered critically how far Chomsky's claim is acceptable. In this context I have shown that there are certain standard assumptions of knowledge which Chomsky's alleged knowledge of language does not fulfil. I have also taken into account some weaker versions of knowledge as formulated particularly by Fodor and, arguably, Wittgenstein and Merleau-Ponty, and have shown that Chomsky's native speakers cannot claim to "know" language even on these weaker assumptions.

# 4

# Chomsky and Private Language

## I

### Contention of Chomsky

In the previous chapter, we have tried to show some of the difficulties that Chomsky's account of knowledge of language or mental representation or internalization of rules involve. We have tried to show how Chomsky's knowledge of language violates our criteria for knowledge in the standard or paradigmatic sense, and how the different attempts to defend Chomsky's stance fails in the long run. Now Chomsky's account of internalization of rules also poses another problem, the problem of privacy. The problem arises in connection with Chomsky's explicit insistence that a language is a purely individual possession. He writes:

> The term "language" as used in ordinary discourse involves obscure socio-political and normative factors. It is doubtful that we can give a coherent account of how the term is actually used. This is not a problem for the ordinary use of language. Its conditions require only that usage be sufficiently clear for ordinary purposes. But in pursuing a serious inquiry into language we require some conceptual precision and therefore must refine, modify or simply replace the concepts of ordinary usage, just as physics assigns a precise technical meaning to such terms as "energy", "force", and "work", departing from

> the imprecise and rather obscure concepts of ordinary usage. It may be possible ... to undertake the study of language in its socio-political dimensions, but this further inquiry can proceed only to the extent that we have some grasp of the properties and principles of a language in a narrower sense, in the sense of individual psychology. – 1988: 37

Thus, Chomsky's primary emphasis is on "individual psychology" to account for language. That is why he observes:

> I should mention that I am using the term "language" to refer to an individual phenomenon, a system represented in the mind/brain of a particular individual. If we could investigate in sufficient details, we would find that no two individuals share exactly the same language in this sense, even identical twins who grow up in the same social environment. Two individuals can communicate to the extent that their languages are sufficiently similar. – Ibid.: 36

The implication of the above accent of Chomsky on language in the sense of *individual psychology* or *as a system represented in the mind/brain of a particular individual* is obvious. Language becomes the individual possession of a particular speaker, and a study of language "will be a study of how the systems represented in the mind/brains of various interacting speakers differ .... " (Ibid.: 37)

This is the sense in which Chomsky would consider language private. Language is private in the sense that it is individual speaker's language; each speaker possesses a different language, i.e. has internalized a different set of rules. Now if language is an individual speaker's language, there is nothing like publicly shared language. This is how Chomsky looks at language. According to him, there is no theoretically interesting concept of language in between those of language (L), i.e. universal, innately, i.e. neutrally or cerebrally categorized principles which all speakers of any language possess and the individual languages of particular speakers (i.e. my or your particular set of syntactic, semantic, etc. rules). Hence terms like "English" or "Italian" refer to nothing in the objective world and certainly cannot have anything of theoretical, explanatory interest. It is just that a number of people in Italy or England have similar languages, and a loose way of indicating this similarity is to say that all speak "English" or "Italian". But strictly speaking, each speaker internalizes a different set of rules, etc. or has a different language. In other words, because speakers of English or Italian have some similarity so that they can communicate with one another to some extent, it is said that they all speak English or Italian. But there is no such language as "English" or "Italian". There is my language or your language or his language – and all these are different languages. Two things, therefore, follow from Chomsky's emphasis on the privacy of individual speaker's language.

(a) In describing and explaining a person's linguistic knowledge, we have no need to speak of a publicly shared language. "This notion [of a public language]", as Chomsky holds, "is unknown to empirical inquiry and raises what seems to be irresoluble problems" (Wiggins 1997: 499).[1]

(b) The speaker follows the rules which are unique to him. (We shall, however, deal with this point later on in this chapter.)

Here we confine our attention to (a) and consider it critically. When Chomsky calls language private, he emphasizes that it is not "a social object, a public thing", in the words of Wiggins (ibid.); it is on the contrary to be explained or accounted for in terms of the individual psychology of speakers. But this is the contention that we doubt. We want to argue that language is an institutional fact, and that it is not reducible to the individual psychology of the speakers, i.e. it is not to be taken as what is internalized by a speaker individually. In other words, we want

---

[1] Incidentally, all that we quote from Wiggins is from his this paper.

to argue in favour of social or publicly shared language and want to insist that no account can be given of what it is to know a language which does not make reference to such a shared public language. This point has been powerfully brought out by David Wiggins in one of his recent papers, "Languages as Social Objects" (1997: 499-524). So we shall utilize the contention of Wiggins to our advantage in the following section.

II

### Wiggins on Languages as Social Objects

What Wiggins tries to show is that there are "public" shared languages, that it is not loose and explanatorily idle to refer to the English or Italian language. He remarks:

> ... We have yet to hear the adherents of Chomsky's scepticism concerning public languages furnish an argument that leads persuasively from what they tell us about the specialized language faculties of human beings to the conclusion that speaking a language is no more than a psychological function of individual beings. – Ibid.: 501

On the contrary, as he argues, there is much to be said for public language.

Before we consider his plea for public language, we may incidentally add a few lines to explain what he means by "public" language or language as social object. This follows from his observation that we have no need "to liken the social objects that are particular languages to the natural substances ..." (ibid.: 522). Perhaps we may understand this well in the light of Searle's distinction between brute and institutional facts (1970: 50-52).[2] There is a familiar picture of the world as being constituted by brute facts like, to use Searle's examples, "This stone is next to that stone", "Bodies attract with a force inversely proportional to the square of the distance between

[2] We have faithfully followed the contention of Searle.

them and directly proportional to the product of their mass". To have systematic knowledge of such brute facts constitutes the model of epistemology of the natural sciences and the concepts that the natural sciences employ are mainly physical. But at the same time there are certain facts which, though objective, cannot be accommodated within the picture of brute facts. They are facts like John married Mary, the Brazil football team beat the French football team by three goals to nil, or the Parliament of India passed the Women's Rights Bill. Statements of facts like these are not reducible to statements about physical properties of states of affair. It is true that a marriage ceremony, a football game or a legislative action involve physical movements. But these physical events acquire meaning not in terms of brute facts but "against a background", in the words of Searle, "of certain kinds of institutions" (ibid.: 51). Such facts about marriage or football games are, therefore, institutional facts. They are facts no doubt, but they are not brute facts since they presuppose certain human institutions. It is only under the institution of marriage that certain forms of behaviour count as John's marrying Mary. It is only in terms of the institution of football that certain activities count as Brazil's defeating France or, it is only given the institution of money that a piece of paper is not merely a piece of grey paper but counts as, say, five pound note. Thus, institutional facts derive their life from various institutions. Similarly, language too is an institutional fact or "a social object", as Wiggins would call it. It is not a brute fact or natural object or natural substance. It is an institution governed by rules arrived at by common agreement. It is only given the institution of language that certain expressions mean or refer to such-and-such. Individual speakers speak language only by being trained to participate in or share the social institution of language. They do not each speak just their own language.

Now we may deal with the question: Why should we appeal to public language as explained above? How to support it? Wiggins has formidable reasons for it. He puts his point by holding that just as "a helmsman steers for port" or "a doctor aims to cure", similarly, a speaker uses language in order to communicate, in order to be understood. But he "aims to be understood" not by saying just anything but by saying this and that. And he cannot achieve his end of being understood successfully unless his saying this and not that is sanctioned by public language, unless he can record his saying in public language to such and such an effect. Thus, the contention of Wiggins is clear. It is part of the speaker's intention to say this rather than that, to go on record as saying in English that such-and-such.

Again, very crucially the argument of Wiggins for public language is backed by normative consideration. He holds that

> if we omit from the account of linguistic communication all mention of the language in which speech is conducted, if we take this piece from out of our philosophy of language [as Chomsky does], then the linguist leaves no locus at all for normative considerations. ... – 1997: 522

He also refers to the same normative consideration elsewhere in the paper. As he observes:

> ... a particular language, ... with all its achievements and latent resources, is something that influences normatively, by its palpable presence in the social world, the linguistic strivings of children, adults, foreigners, poets, writers, politicians and the rest. – Ibid.: 500

As just noted, consideration of normative factors is very important, since they have no meaning unless there is a publicly shared language. In other words, without a public language we have no locus for judging whether our utterances are correct, apt or inept, significant, accurate or excellent. Unless we assume the existence of English, etc. there is no way to identify mistakes which most or all people make, no way to determine "seriously and objectively that such and such an utterance is apt or inept, well-made or ill-made, or not in good English". For, according to Wiggins, a person speaks incorrectly not because he differs from others but because he violates the English institution which is the standard.

To sum up crudely, whether a speaker communicates successfully or whether his saying is apt or inept is "answerable" to the public language itself. It is in the light of this conviction for publicly shared language that Wiggins looks at John Foster and Crispin Wright and evaluate their contentions. Foster (1976) writes:

> Rather than ask for a statement of the knowledge implicit in linguistic competence, let us ask for a statement of a theory [the] knowledge of which would suffice for such competence. ... The theory reveals the semantic machinery which competence works, but leaves undetermined the psychological form in which competence exists.
>
> – Quoted from Wiggins 1997: 506

In the above passages, Foster seems to highlight that, contrary to Chomsky's view, the linguists should focus on the rules, etc. of a language like English or Italian, and not on the speaker's psychology. Wiggins endorses this point (though he differs from Foster in some respects), since it confirms his thought that language is not confined to the individual psychology (implicit competence) of the speaker but works as publicly shared language.

Wiggins is, however, critical about Wright's emphasis on a community of speakers without acknowledging the existence of public language to which the community of speakers conform. Wright (1986/1991) argues that if the way in which the speakers function is not taken into account, then it

> generates an intolerable [division] between the concepts of meaning and understanding: [for] truths about meaning have

> to be, ultimately, constituted by facts about understanding. So to aspire to a theory which aims to describe semantic machinery independently of any assumptions about what speakers know is to aspire to theory with no proper subject matter. – Quoted from Wiggins 1997: 509

Again he points out:

> I do not think we can attach any content to the supposition that [an expression] has a meaning except in so far as meaning is thought of as constituted, at least in part, by convention; and I do not think we can attain to an account of the distinction between a convention and a corresponding regularity except by invoking the idea of practitioners' intention, qualified in various ways, to uphold that regularity. [Thus] the proper standing of the axioms of a theory of meaning must, it would seem, be grounded in speakers' intentions. ... – Ibid.

Thus, the kernel of his contention is that a proper study of language should be a study of speakers and speakers' understanding and intentions.

On Wiggins' view, though Wright is correct in making reference to a community of speakers, yet he gives a wrong account of how exactly reference to a community of speakers should enter into characterizing individual speaker's knowledge of rules, etc. The way Wright proposes his thesis is as follows. Why is it that a term like "red" has the sense that it has? His answer is that "red" is employed only with respect to things that are red and not not-red because of a convention, or regularity or habit in a population *G* to conform to this rule, and because the speakers in *G* are disposed to expect that others also follow the same rule. So on his view no reference need be made to "public" shared language. He would rather appeal to the habits, expectations, etc. of individuals. According to him, it seems that a language is defined in terms of the similar habits, dispositions, etc. of members of a community or culture. Wiggins responds to the Wright thesis in the following way. This accent on speakers, their intentions, habits or dispositions is wrong. In fact, how to identify the speakers? Can we do so by their religion or genetic make-up? Do we not place the speakers by the language they speak? In other words, there is, according to Wiggins, no way of specifying or identifying the community whose habits the individual speaker conforms to except as the community of speakers of, say, the English language. The reason why speakers use "red" to refer to red things only is not that each believes that most people call red things "red", but that this is the way of speaking in English. Therefore, reference to "public" shared language is ineliminable; it is not reducible to individual psychology as advocated by Chomsky and Wright.

Thus, the contention of Wiggins is very clear. To sum up, he points out that no account can be given of what it is to know a language which does not refer to a shared public language. When linguists specify rules, etc. they are not, contrary to Chomsky's or Wright's view, describing the psychology (individual or social) of speakers, but the public and social institution we call "Italian" or "English" or whatever. Facts about psychology may explain how people manage to know a language, but should not enter into any serious account of language or knowledge of language. Knowledge of a language is the ability to produce and understand sentences "that have currency or acceptance in that language". If this is so, knowledge of a language cannot be explained in terms of Chomsky's individual psychology or individual internalization of rules, etc. or Crispin Wright's habits, dispositions or expectations of individual speakers. Needless to say, this contention of Wiggins is very important and deserves our special attention. It suggests Quine's point, which we have already made use of in our previous chapter, about the indeterminacy in identifying the alleged "inner" rules which Chomsky thinks we know or the Wittgensteinian idea about the very notion of a rule requiring a reference to the practices which determine how the rule is applied and hence what it really amounts to a point we shall take up in the subsequent section.

Further, Wiggins' argument crucially substantiates our contention against Chomsky's individual speaker's language. Strictly speaking, Chomsky's account of competence or knowledge of language ignores a social, interpersonal dimension. If what Chomsky says about "Italian", etc. is correct, then no reference to a shared language is necessary in specifying what it is to know a language, for there are as many languages as there are people. In principle, it would seem for Chomsky, a person could know a language, i.e. have internalized a set of syntactic, semantic rules without knowing anything at all how other people speak. For the language one knows is as it is represented in one's individual mind/brain. Hence, for it is at most a contingent fact that acquiring one's language is done through interpersonal engagement with other speakers. But Chomsky seems to flog the wrong horse. For someone who knows a language knows not a language which is peculiar to him. If there is only my language, your language or his language, we doubt whether Chomsky can handle the problem of communication seriously and can account for the objective basis of judging that such and such utterance is apt or inept. It is, therefore, more reasonable to equate knowledge of language with knowledge of a public language or dialect thereof such as English or Geordie English or Pidgin English, and to know that is necessarily to know a great deal about the behaviour of others. To know, e.g. the meaning of "red" is not simply to associate "red" with red things in one's own, as it were, private dictionary, but to know that "red" is used by speakers of English (though not speakers of France) to denote red things.

## III

### Private Rule-following

Chomsky's emphasis on individual speaker's language not

only means that there cannot be any public language but also may mean, a speaker follows rules which are not accessible to others. If privacy in the second sense is an implication of Chomsky's view, then we can profitably draw on discussions of Wittgenstein's philosophy to question it. In fact, Wittgenstein has powerfully argued that any idea of private language or private rule following is, in the words of Kripke, "insane and intolerable" (1982: 60).[3] We shall now try to develop the fundamental contention of Wittgenstein. It should be mentioned here, however, that Wittgenstein's position is variously interpreted. In Kripke's interpretation of him, communal practices are necessary in order for it to make sense to say that someone is following rules or means this rather than that by his words. But this interpretation has been challenged by lots of writers like McGinn (1984: chap. 2) Still if Wittgenstein is saying what Kripke thinks he is, and if this is a plausible thing to say, then it can be an effective weapon against Chomsky's view of language where the individual follows his own unique syntactic and semantic rules. It is not, however, important for our purposes whether Kripke's interpretation of Wittgenstein is correct: the important thing is that Kripke's point about the role of community in rule following is a serious one with implications for Chomsky – whether or not it is a point correctly ascribed to Wittgenstein himself.

Wittgenstein, as Kripke understands him, points out that when we say, "we mean addition by plus", e.g. (or generally follow this rule), it has perfect sense, and that this perfect sense of our rule-following is derived from custom. He explicitly refers to custom in the following way:

> I have further indicated that a person goes by a sign-post only in so far as there exists a regular use of sign posts, a custom.
>
> – Wittgenstein 1953: 80

[3] We have mainly followed Kripke's interpretation.

Or:

> It is not possible that there should have been only one occasion on which someone obeyed a rule. It is not possible there should have been only one occasion on which a report was made, an order given or understood, and so on. To obey a rule, to make a report, to give an order, to play a game of chess are customs (uses, institutions). – Ibid.: 81

So the point of Wittgenstein is that our rule following is governed or confirmed by custom or regular and established practice. According to him, at least on Kripke's reading, the very notion of rules requires reference to common practices which determine how the rule is applied, and hence what the rule amounts to. If this is so, it will not allow any solitary individual to mean anything or follow any rule all by himself. Consequently, there cannot be private language or private rule following.

Let us consider what someone means by a certain symbol (say "plus") or what he is doing in following the rule behind it. What he means is evident from the fact that, situation when asked for the sum of "60" and "25", he unhesitatingly replies by answering "85 ".

We do respond to question what is the sum of 60 + 25? in a similar way without any thought. We do so without any strict justification. We can say nothing except that this is what we do. Nonetheless we act unhesitatingly and with confidence, unreflectingly or blindly. As Wittgenstein puts it, "when I obey a rule, I do not choose. I obey the rule blindly" (ibid.: 85). I obey the rule blindly since I cannot support my rule – following by appealing to any conclusive evidence, say, in terms of any fact about me. Yet this does not disturb my confidence that I am not wrong. It is a part of rule-following that to mean a symbol (e.g. plus) in a certain way, or respond (e.g. 85 to the sum of 60 and 25) in a particular way is the right way of doing things.

It is true that for Wittgenstein and Kripke, there cannot

be a private rule-follower. But for the sake of argument let us imagine that there can be a private rule-follower. Now the private rule-follower may also be confident about his unique rule-following, though there is no conclusive justification for it. What is then the distinction between a private rule-follower who follows alike rule and the rule-follower just mentioned above who follows the rule of addition? They are equally sure about their respective rule-following. They are equally blind. Is it that they stand on the same ground? To be sure, Wittgenstein would not approve of this kind of deliberation. He would insist that our rule-following has no meaning unless we can make a distinction between "I am following a rule" and "I am under the impression that I am following a rule". The impression that I follow a rule does not confirm that I really follow the rule unless there is something, some criterion that proves my impression correct, makes my impression legitimate or justified. A private rule-follower by definition is confined to his own rule, to his own unique way of meaning things. He cannot claim that this is what everybody will mean or follow under similar condition, that this is supported by ordinary, common practice. He has no criterion outside of his own impression to decide whether his rule-following is correct or misplaced, whether he really does so or merely thinks himself to be doing so. Hence, he is not strictly following a rule. He obeys the rule only according to his choice. He is confined only to what appeals to him or strikes him. That is why Wittgenstein observes:

> To think one is obeying a rule is not to obey a rule. Hence it is not possible to obey a rule "privately"; otherwise thinking one was obeying a rule would be the same thing as obeying it.
> – 1953: 81

But this is not the case with a rule-follower who follows the rule, e.g. of addition. He does not merely choose to obey the rule according to his own sweet will. Nor can he do so. There is a check or constraint in his case to determine whether he is genuinely obeying a rule or merely thinks he is doing it. This check or constraint, this criterion comes from community and its practice based on common agreement and sharing a common form of life. Let us try to explain this. If we consider an individual as a member of a community, others can judge whether he is following a rule correctly or incorrectly. Others will then furnish, in the words of Kripke,

> justification conditions for attributing correct or incorrect rule-following to the subject, and these will not be simply that the subject's own authority is unconditionally to be accepted.
>
> – 1982: 89

Thus, according to Wittgenstein, on Kripke's account, the concept of a rule derives its life from the uniform practices of a community. To take one example from Kripke, consider a little boy learning addition. If the boy says that the sum of 68 and 57 is 5, the teacher would inevitably think that he is not adding and would take him to task for that. He would judge that the boy is not following the rule correctly as he and others like him would do. Similarly, if an adult, who usually adds correctly or whom I judge to be doing things exactly as I would do, suddenly begins to say that the sum of 68 and 57 is 5, I at once judge that he is not following the rule as he used to do it before. I begin to suspect whether he is now in his senses.

Thus emerges the condition under which one can assert "I mean addition by plus". He can do so not in terms of his own individual impressions or intuitions but only in virtue of its getting endorsement from others in the community. If his response does not fulfil the expectation of others, he cannot be said to be following a rule, or at least the relevant rule. In fact, our community has uniform practices regarding addition or anything else. The only way to judge or check that an individual has learned a concept, the concept of "plus" for example, is by looking at whether his response agrees with those of others in the community, whether, e.g. when asked for the sum of 60 and

25, he responds 85. If an individual is not a member of a society, or does not interact with a community, if he formulates rules or means things all by himself, and thereby deviates from the norm prevalent in or accepted by a community, we cannot judge that he is following a rule; we cannot understand what he means by such-and-such a symbol and nor can he. It is community practice that decides or justifies what it is to follow a rule, or mean such-and-such by such-and-such a symbol on a given occasion. If an individual does not respond 125 when asked for the sum of 68 and 57, and in other cases fails to conform with a public practice, we cannot assert that he means addition by plus.

For Chomsky, knowing a rule of syntax or semantics is a matter of being in a certain mental state, of having "internalized" a rule. The question which Kripke emphasizes is: On what basis can it be said that a person is following one rule rather than another? What is it which shows that a speaker is, say, following a plus, rather than a quus, rule and so means addition by "plus", rather than something else? Kripke's central claim, which he thinks he finds in Wittgenstein, is that nothing whatsoever about the current state of the speaker (e.g. his current mental imagery, his reciting some rule to himself, a flash of intuition, or whatever) can show that he is a plus rather than a quus speaker. Suppose, e.g. the speaker could recite the rule and say that is the rule he is following. But reciting a rule does not establish what the correct application of it will be. Whatever the rule recited, the speaker could claim that applying it in this way, rather than that, constitutes a correct application. For example, the quus speaker will claim that the way he goes on is the way demanded by the rule he can recite. The only thing that shows that we are following the plus rule – that we mean addition *b* "plus" – is that we go on in certain ways rather than others. For Kripke, it is only because we go on in these ways – because there is communal agreement – that we can say that doing this, rather than doing that, is what the rule for "plus" requires.

The upshot of such considerations will be that we cannot conceive of the speaker as someone who might, conceivably, have not been part of linguistic community at all; as someone who magically or by luck came to be equipped with a Chomskyan internalized knowledge of the rules of his language. It is not that this person would be speaking a private language, following private rules. Rather, he would not be speaking at all, he would be following no rules. For the conditions would be missing which are required for distinguishing his following the rule correctly and it merely seeming to him that he is. This, as we will see in Chapter 5, poses a special problem for Chomsky's theory according to which some rules, i.e. the "innate" ones of "universal" grammar are not acquired through social interaction.

To put it in a different way, if knowing one's language is an internal state of the speaker, then it seems to be logically possible that such knowledge could be acquired and possessed by a speaker who has no relationship to other speakers. The problem then arises as to whether this speaker could then be said to know his language at all. Assuming this alleged knowledge takes the form, in large part, of knowing the rules for ordering and applying words or other linguistic elements, the problem becomes that of whether there can be genuine rule-following going on in the case of such a speaker. How will one make the distinction between applying the rule correctly and its merely seeming to the speaker that it is being applied correctly? In practice, of course, the speaker will be a member of a community, but that does not remove the problem. For, on Chomsky's model of linguistic knowledge, the speaker's manifest linguistic behaviour is not the criterion for his knowing a language, but at best evidence for this. Hence, the logical possibility remains that the rules the speaker allegedly knows may be different from anything that manifests itself in linguistic behaviour. Whether this is a logical possibility is just what is in question. Compare this the possibility, rejected by Wittgenstein, that what the speaker means by sensation words like "pain" is something that is only contingently connected with overt behaviour.

It follows from the foregoing that Wittgenstein uses three fundamental concepts in his account of rule-following. These are: (a) agreement, (b) form of life, and (c) criteria.

AGREEMENT

We generally mean such-and-such by such-and such a symbol. We respond uniformly under similar conditions, we generally mean addition by plus. We respond similarly when required to calculate the sum of 68 and 57. But there is no objective guarantee, no objective fact prior to and independent of our practices to establish conclusively that we cannot do otherwise.Yet this does not prevent us from doing things which we are accustomed to do and expecting that others will behave similarly under similar conditions. Our uniform response or uniform expectation is not due to any contribution by such objective "facts", but is simply a "brute fact" (to use Kripke's terminology): the brute fact that we agree with each other in our responses and expectations.

FORM OF LIFE

This common agreement is "not an agreement", as Wittgenstein observes, "in opinions but in form of life" (1953: 24). The notion of "form of life" is very important, though a complicated one. Roughly it means "the consensus of linguistic and non-linguistic assumptions and activities, natural propensities or dispositions" which "humans as social beings share with one another" (Grayling 1988: 84). It is this consensus of the outlook, assumptions and practices that is woven into language and gives it its life. It is this concordance that activates the practice of a community and is expressed in agreement in judgements and behaviour. If a private language speaker speaks, we cannot understand him. For his language is confined to his mental horizon and is not exposed to the form of life, i.e. linguistic and non-linguistic practice, natural dispositions that we share and approve of as members of a community. Thus, it is form of life that provides the ultimate framework which issues in common agreement as to what it is one means by a symbol on a given occasion, what it is to follow a rule genuinely under given conditions, as well as its role and utility in our life. When we reach this framework, nothing more is needed. "What has to be accepted, the given is – so one could say – forms of life" (Wittgenstein 1953: 226).

CRITERIA

The role of criteria is very crucial, since without it there is nothing to determine or check whether one is following a rule genuinely or correctly. When a child, in the presence of a chair, says "This is a table", others do not endorse him. For he is not using the term "table" in conformity with practice. But if he says, "This is a chair", he is following the rule correctly since it is endorsed by the elders. Thus, the criterion of correct rule-following is provided by a community.

We may now summarize the fundamental points of Wittgenstein's contention on Kripke's interpretation. Wittgenstein highlights what we are to understand by "rule" and "rule following" by giving the example of a sign-post. The function of the sign-post is to indicate what direction to take. We follow the guidance of the sign-post only because of the fact that there is a custom, a practice which determines how we shall look at the sign-post. As Wittgenstein puts it (already quoted), "... a person goes by a sign-post in so far as there exists a regular use of sign-posts, a custom". This is exactly the sense in which we shall take "rule" in the case of language: A rule stands there like a sign-post. Since a rule-like, a sign-post is based on custom or regular and established use, it is not possible that there is only one occasion on which one obeys a rule.

This accent on custom draws our attention to the following important facts. First, rule following is not a hidden mental activity, but is something public. When someone sees a sign-post and follows the relevant direction, it is not that he is internally following a rule and then behaving according to it as a casual result of the "internal" rule-following. His going by the sign-post is his following the rule. Rule-following is just what is expressed in our habitual practice: it does not involve any mysterious mental act. Second, "obeying a rule is a practice", the practice of a community. A rule is an institution. That is, rules that we follow are not imposed on us from any objective fact outside; they are established by common agreement in the community within the background of a shared form of life. Rules and agreement are therefore interrelated.

> The word "agreement" and the word "rule" are related to one another, they are cousins. If I teach anyone the use of the one word, he learns the use of the other with it.
>
> – Wittgenstein 1953: 86

In fact, it is this communal agreement that determines, provides the check or criterion as to whether we are really following rules or merely think that we are doing so. An individual follows a rule if it is in keeping with the regularity that exists in a community, the regularity that is sanctioned by it. Hence, there is no sense in private rule-following since it does not correspond to the practice prevalent in a society.

If there is an individual who follows the rules that lie exclusively in his head, there cannot be any objective criterion of correctness of his rule following. "Whatever", as Wittgenstein puts it, "is going to seem right to me is right" (ibid.: 92). Let us explain this point a little. If the language that I speak is my own, I know from my own case what, e.g. "pain" means. "I know only what I call that, not what anyone else does." It is also not possible for me to teach others what this word means to me, for in doing that successfully I must have to know that the man whom I teach applies the word to the right private object. But if all of us have their own respective languages and rules, I cannot know that.

For, it may be possible that you use the word "pain" to refer to sensation that I do not do; it may also be possible that perhaps you do not use the word "pain" to refer to any sensation at all. If this is so, what I can know is only how I use a word to designate a particular object. But, if any word, referential or otherwise, is to have a meaning, there must be a rule governing its use or application, and this rule must provide the basis of checking whether the rule is followed or whether the word is used aptly, appropriately and correctly. The question is whether the unique rule-following of an individual speaker meets this condition. We think it does not. The only way to decide or check whether any use of a word is correct or consistent or appropriate is to see whether my use agrees with that of others. But this will be to appeal to a common language which will be the locus of how everyone should use a word. Since this language has been given up, I shall have to decide whether I use a word appropriately only in terms of my language that I speak. I cannot go any further than saying that whatever is going to seem right to me is right. This means, we have no objective basis of judging whether my utterance is right or not. Consequently, as Wittgenstein puts it, "we can't talk about right" (1953: 92).

One may, however, retort that the private rule-follower can indeed check whether he uses the word "pain" (or follows the rule that this is to be called "pain") consistently by remembering that he did so in a similar way in the past. But this will not do. In fact, to err is human, and we sometimes make memory errors. How then to distinguish between genuine and erroneous memory? How then can I distinguish real remembering from merely believing that I am remembering the way I used a word in the past? One may reply that I can do so by checking one memory-impression by another memory-impression, for example, I can determine whether I remember rightly the time of departure of a train by recalling an image of a page of the time-table. But "this process has got to produce a memory which is actually correct. If the mental image of the time-table could not itself be tested for correctness, how could it confirm the correctness of the first memory" (Ibid.: 93-94).

In other words, how can one memory-impression confirm another memory-impression? This will be like buying several copies of the morning paper to check or confirm whether what was read in the first copy is true. Strictly speaking, we can judge the correctness of memory-impression only by reference to a standard outside of memory-impression, for example, in the case of the train's departure, by actually consulting the time-table or by talking to the relevant authority on the phone.

All that is said in the foregoing is only to highlight that a speaker cannot be the final arbiter of what he says, of what rules he follows. The mandate must come from outside of him and his rule-following. There must be a criterion to evaluate whether he is really following a rule or is merely under the impression of doing so. This criterion comes from community practice. It is the common agreement existing in a community that determines what rules to follow, what to mean by expressions under given conditions. Hence, in the case of a private speaker, we cannot decide or judge whether he is following the rule. Since we are uncertain about that, we cannot also understand what he means by using a certain expression, whether he speaks sensibly. It goes without saying that the alleged private language of Chomsky is unconnected with the common practice, with the institution of language and so we cannot understand a private speaker.

# 5

# On Chomsky's Commitment to Innateness Thesis

## I

In this chapter, we shall deal with Chomsky's innateness hypothesis and consider how far this innateness is acceptable.

According to Chomsky, for a child to acquire knowledge of its language, it must innately know the principles and categories of Universal Grammar. Now if there is innate knowledge, it will be knowledge that the child possesses independently of its relations with other speakers. This is because it is knowledge possessed prior to such relations.[1] If Chomsky's innateness hypothesis is accepted, then it follows that at least some linguistic knowledge is "a-social". Once it is conceded that some such knowledge is "a-social", it is unclear why we should resist the conclusion that knowledge of one's language at large is something that might be obtained independently of communal participation. Hence, it is important – if the general direction of our argument towards

---

1 Strictly speaking, the mere fact that my knowledge of *X* is innate does not entail that it was not learned or taught to me by others. For, may be, as Plato suggested in Meno, it is knowledge I acquired in a previous life. Clearly, though, this is not a possibility that Chomsky contenances.

the social and interpersonal is to be sustained – to examine and challenge Chomsky's innateness hypothesis.

This hypothesis is not, of course, an incidental aspect of Chomsky's overall position. On the contrary, it plays a vital role in his explanation of how linguistic competence is possible. We shall now take up this very question. One may reasonably wonder how a child or a native speaker comes to possess complicated knowledge with ease, whether this knowledge (competence) is entirely acquired through experience, or whether it is partly an innate possession. Chomsky, in his account of competence, takes note of such question, and the way he tackles them leads, as just noted before, to innateness hypothesis, i.e. to the thesis that knowledge of the rules of a language which constitutes the competence of a child or a native speaker is ultimately derived from some innately possessed organizing principles of the mind.

## II

We may, however, ponder as to what is so conspicuous in the nature of competence or in the process of language acquisition that may lead Chomsky to postulate the innateness hypothesis. Chomsky would respond to this in the following manner. We cannot doubt that the rules a child internalizes (and thereby becomes a competent speaker in its language) are not taught explicitly and it is extremely doubtful whether it is at all possible to teach a child all these rules. Nor can we say that the child internalizes on the basis of abstraction and generalization from the observable features spoken by the adults of its community. Then what is the plausible alternative? According to Chomsky, it is to admit that the child itself constructs the rules. But how can it be done? In reply to this question, Chomsky holds that we must keep in mind the complexity of the structure of language that a child has to master. He draws our attention to the fact that the complexity of the structure of any language points to the complexity of the underlying system of rules. Now he holds that a child can normally acquire mastery of his language; and the ease with which it acquires its mastery indicates that it does not find these rules complex and difficult to learn. Therefore, a theory of language-acquisition should explain how a child can have mastery or competence over the rules of its language so easily in spite of the complexity of rules. Chomsky claims that it can be explained adequately by recognizing the innate language acquisition device which is equipped with the universal principles of language or linguistic universals. This explains why the child can itself construct the rules. It can do so since it is innately endowed with the universal principles of language. Hence, Chomsky observes:

> We must ... develop as rich a hypothesis concerning linguistic universals as can be supported by available evidence. This specification can then be attributed to the system AD as an intrinsic property. – 1966: 11

It follows from the above belief that linguistic universals, for Chomsky, are innate. This implies that innateness is, for him, the best explanation of linguistic universals. Let us now elaborate how Chomsky argues for it. We may try to substantiate his contention by considering one example of linguistic universals, viz. that rules are structure dependent (needless to say, this will apply to all cases of linguistic universals). Chomsky (1988: 41-45) tells us to imagine a Martian scientist, John M., who wants to know about human language. Observing the speakers of Spanish, he discovers that they utter sentences like:

(1) a. *El hombre está en la casa.*
The man is in the house.

b. *El hombre está content.*
The man is happy.

(2) *El hombre, que está contento, está en la casa.*
The man, who is happy, is in the house.

He further discovers that they form interrogative sentences corresponding to (1) by placing the verb in front of the sentence such as:

(3) a. *Está el hombre en la casa*?
Is the man in the house?

b. *Está el hombre contento*?
Is the man happy?

Let us call this rule *R* which consists in moving "the first occurrence of the verbal form *esta* (or others like it)", "to the front of the sentence". Now suppose John M. thinks that *R* will apply to all cases of interrogative formation. He would then follow *R* in the case of (3), viz.

(4) *Está el hombre, que contento, está en la casa*?
Is the man, who happy, is at home?

But he would soon find that this sentence is not approved of in Spanish or in English. Actually the correct form is:

(5) *Está el hombre, que esta contento, en la casa*?
Is the man, who is happy, at home?

Let us call this correct rule *R-Q* which is the structure-dependent rule.

Again, the Martian scientist, if a serious one, will discover that *R-Q* is more complex than the simple linear rule *R* that he has discarded and that even a child employs *R-Q*, though it is more complex than *R*. So we may reasonably ask: why is it the case that the child makes use of the more complex rule instead of the simple one? One of the possible explanations may be that the child has been taught to do so by its parents. Then the explanation will amount to this. Children proceed inductively, just like John M. From the observation of examples like (1) and (3), they pick up the simple linear rule *R* as the operative rule. This prompts them to (4). But when they are told by their parents that they should say not (4) but (5), they at last learn the rule *R-Q*. In this way, learning to employ *R-Q* is ultimately a matter of instruction and correction. But Chomsky does not accept this. According to him, children never make mistakes about the formation of proper interrogative sentences like a Martian scientist, and "not receive corrections or instructions about them". He observes:

> It is certainly absurd to argue that the children are trained to use the structure-dependent rule. In fact, the problem never arises in language learning. A person may go through a considerable part of his life without ever facing relevant evidence, but he will have no hesitation in using the structure-dependent rule. – 1976: 32

If an explanation of a child's devising the structure-dependent rule in terms of training, instruction or correction is wholly redundant, then the innatist explanation begins to look very promising. We may say with emphasis and confidence that the child possesses this linguistic universal (or others like it) innately.

To recapitulate, in the words of Chomsky:

> The child learning Spanish or any other human language knows, in advance of experience, that the rules will be structure dependent. The child does not consider the simple linear rule *R*, then discards it in favour of more complex rule *R-Q*, in the manner of the rational scientist enquiring into language. Rather, the child knows without experience or instruction that the linear rule *R* is not a candidate and that the structure-dependent rule *R-Q* is the only possibility. This knowledge is part of the child's biological endowment, part of the structure of language faculty. – 1988: 45

Thus, as we can see now, all human languages (not only Spanish but also English or any other language) employ some basic rules, structure-dependent rules, for example. It is employment of these basic rules or linguistic universals that contributes to the basic similarity of all languages in spite of their surface differences. The best way to explain these linguistic universals, according to Chomsky, is to say that we possess them innately from our very birth. This also explains why the child can acquire competence in any language, depending on the linguistic community to which it belongs.

Chomsky's famous argument for the innateness hypothesis is the argument from poverty of stimulus. We shall now try to develop this point in some detail. The poverty of the stimulus argument, as Ramsey and Stich point out (1990: 181), admits of three versions.[2] The first version is what they would call "The Argument for Minimal Nativism". According to this version, a child is "exposed to only a very impoverished sample of often misleading linguistic data". This poverty of the stimulus appears from the following facts:

(a) The limited data which a child encounters from its linguistic community are rather messy. They often involve idiosyncratic, ungrammatical sentences, incomplete sentences, false starts, change of plan in mid-course and so on.

(b) Further, the child does not know many things about language that a linguist knows. It does not know, like a richly informed linguist, that certain sentences are grammatical, or that certain sentences are paraphrases of certain others, etc. Hence, it has no access to many kinds of linguistic data to decide between competing grammars.

Yet, out of the limited and messy data, the child can very well internalize a language or grammar which a video tape-recorder or a puppy is unable to do, even if it is exposed to the primary linguistic data. This gap between input and output can be bridged only by ascribing to the child a learning mechanism

---

[2] In this connection, we should note that we owe much to this paper in explaining the three versions of the poverty of the stimulus argument (pp. 177-205).

which it innately possesses before the acquisition begins. The reason why a video tape-recorder cannot have any internally represented grammar is that it lacks the sophisticated innate learning mechanism of the cognitive system which a child has. In the words of Chomsky:

> ... it is clear that the language each person acquires is a rich and complex construction hopelessly under-determined by the fragmentary evidence available ... this fact can be explained only on the assumption that these individuals employ highly restrictive principles that guide the construction of grammar. – 1980a: 134

The crucial point that this version of the poverty of the stimulus argument highlights is that the child's innate learning mechanism or sophisticated cognitive system, to do its job, must have a "strong bias" for acquiring certain grammar as against others. For the data from which the child has acquired its grammar can also at the same time be taken care of by an indefinitely large class of grammars, many of which the child will reject at the time of attaining its grammars. In other words, the acquisition mechanism must be able to pick up the grammar that is approved of by its community vis-à-vis the other grammars that are equally compatible with the data. Thus, the thesis of minimal nativism simply emphasizes this bias in favour of a certain grammar and against others – the bias that is entertained by the language acquisition of the child with an innate learning mechanism.

We know that a significant aspect of Chomsky is his departure from the empiricist conception of mind. And we may think that he has succeded in undermining the empiricist conception of mind with this accent on strongly biased innate learning mechanism. But this is not true. For even the rigid empiricist will not deny that learning involves sophisticated innate mechanisms and biases. Even an empiricist, as Quine observes, is knowingly and cheerfully up to his neck in innate mechanisms of learning readiness (Searle 1974: 22). If Chomsky is willing to counter empiricist accounts of mind that is one of his significant objectives, he must have to say something more about the nature of these innate mechanisms and biases.

This leads to the second version of the poverty of the stimulus argument which Ramsey and Stich call "the argument against empiricism". Let us try to develop this argument. Prima facie, it may appear that argument against all empiricist accounts of mind is not possible. For even if Chomsky can effectively demonstrate that one or another specific empiricist theory cannot explain how the mind produces the right grammar on the basis of the primary linguistic data, he cannot prevent the "resourceful empiricist" from developing another theory in keeping with empiricist principles which can accomplish the task. Chomsky however has a powerful strategy to combat all empiricist theories. This strategy may be called "the competent scientist gambit". The basic point of this gambit is this. We can think of a learning mechanism which is the most powerful that an empiricist can dream of, and then can show that such a learning mechanism fails to do what the child is capable of. If we can do this, we can have final say against all kinds of empiricism. The learning mechanism Chomsky speaks of refers to a very competent scientist.

Let us see whether a scientist can do what a child can – whether he can discover the right grammar from limited and inadequate data. How will he go on? He will collect data, give sophisticated data analysis, formulate imaginative hypotheses on the basis of the data available to him. He will utilize the methodological resource "typically employed in empirical theory construction and selection". Yet he will not be able to learn the language or find the right grammar from the given linguistic data. Surely, he is intelligent and creative: he can definitely think up a large variety of grammars. But he cannot select the right or correct grammar from them as a child does. To show this, let us imagine a pair of grammars with the following characteristics:

i. Both these grammars make essentially the same judgements about linguistic phenomena that "show up" in the primary linguistic data.
ii. Both of them are intuitively simple.

Confronted with these two different grammars, the scientist cannot do what the child can. He cannot choose between the grammars as the child does so easily. He fails because of the following reasons. Since both the two grammars are equally compatible with the data, the data themselves cannot help him rule one out and choose the correct grammar. Again, since both of them are intuitively simple, methodological consideration too does not show him the way out. If this is the case, then the empiricist conception of mind is too poor to account for language learning or acquiring the right grammar. Now clearly this anti-empiricist claim works negatively about language learning. So this must be supplemented by a positive thesis.

This is well attended to by the third or final version of the poverty of the stimulus argument, which Ramsey and Stich call "the argument of rationalism". We shall now consider this final version. If the empiricist account of the mind is of no avail regarding language learning, what is the theory of mind to which we can hopefully look? If we address this question, we must first recall exactly where the empiricist fails. Strictly speaking, the problem for the component scientist *qua* empiricist is not that he cannot think up the right grammar. Indeed, he can do so, being clever, creative and resourceful as he really is. The real problem is much deeper. It is that he can also think up other grammars which are equally simple and equally compatible with the primary linguistic data; and he has no clue how to choose between the alternative grammars. On the face of it, we can take the following promising step to resolve this problem.

Let us suppose that all the humanly learnable languages which can be mentally represented have certain properties in common. Now, if the scientist is already enlightened about the universal features of all languages or grammars, it will help him greatly and narrow down "the search space". Then he will be able to rule out those grammars which do not share the features – the features that impose constraint on all human languages or grammars. This is actually what the child does. He is endowed with a richly innate information about language, with genetically coded principles that put a limit to all human languages. These principles are triggered by environment, however impoverished it may be. And, consequently, the child is able to choose the right grammar or acquire competence, i.e. knowledge of language.

This contention of Chomsky obviously goes beyond what any empiricist theory of mind can endorse. As Searle puts it:

> Chomsky is arguing not simply that the child must have "learning readiness", "bias" and "dispositions", but that he must have a specific set of linguistic mechanisms at work.
>
> – 1974: 22

The final version of the poverty of the stimulus argument draws our attention to the crucial point that a child is unable to discover the right grammar by eliminating other equally compatible grammars without going on with the task with a rich set of innate constraints. The fact that innate learning mechanism contains such constraints is the conclusion to be derived from the final version.

To conclude, we shall try to draw the various threads together to sum up the fundamental points of Chomsky's innateness hypo, he says, are programmed into the child's brain and account for its competence or knowledge of language. This innatist claim draws upon the following points:

(a) the child's ability to master a very complex language with ease and within a short period; and

(b) his ability to have this mastery in spite of the poverty of the data.

But the story is not complete if we do not take into account the recent modularity thesis of Chomsky and Fodor which provides a powerful defence of innateness hypothesis (Chomsky 2000; Smith 1999). According to this thesis, mind is "modular", i.e. "compartmentalized", in the words of Neil Smith, "in such a way that different tasks are subserved by different mechanism" (1999: 17).[3] Sight and smell, taste and touch, language are all distinct from each other. In other words, language faculty is a separate module, a "dedicated input system" (according to Fodor) like all other modules – sight smell, hearing, etc. Like all other modules, language too is specialized for a particular domain; it is "hard wired" with a particular part of the brain dedicated to it, its structure and function are largely innately determined. Chomsky, however, does not share all the ideas of Fodorian modularity. First, language, according to him, is not only an input system in the way vision, for example, is; it is also an output system "geared to the expression and communication of thought". And a part or subsystem of our brain or central system is dedicated to language with these two correlated systems. Second, he does not think, like Fodor, that the central system is essentially unstructured and non-modular. On the contrary, it is, he thinks, intricately structured and also modular in the sense that many of our abilities going beyond purely sensory perception are independent of one another. For example, we have separate mechanisms not only underlying language acquisition and production but also "underlying", in the words of Neil Smith, "our ability to recognize faces, to provide moral judgements and to evaluate social relations" (1999: 20). Not only is there an innate basis of language, but virtually all human

---

[3] In dealing with modularity thesis of Chomsky and Fodor, I depend heavily on Neil Smith's book.

activities like face recognition, analysis of personality and the like appeal to have an innate basis.

It is – not perhaps out of place to consider very briefly how Chomsky's innateness hypothesis is developed by Fodor-Fodor not only argues that language learning and processing faculty are innate, but also that the human representational system or cognitive mechanism is tied to an innate language of thought. Hence, all concepts are innate due to the representational power of the language of thought. And, to learn a language, you need this representational system rich enough to enable you to match Mentalese predicates with the predicates of language you learn. To give an example: [Bear $(x)$] is true (in English) iff $G(x)$ where $G$ is a Mentalese predicate. The child has learned "bear" when he adopts the correct truth rule, when "bear" has the same extension with $G$. Obviously, he learns the meaning of "bear" only in terms of $G$ which is a predicate in the repertoire of his Mentalese. Hence, any predicate that he learns is only a matter of translation from an innate Mentalese counterpart. As Fodor puts it:

> ... one cannot learn a first language unless one already has a system capable of representing the predicates in that language and their extensions. And on the basis of circularity, that system cannot be the language that is learned. Hence, at least some cognitive operations are carried out in languages other than natural languages. My view is that you cannot learn a language unless you have already learned one ... the language of thought is known ... but not learned. That is, it is innate.
>
> – 1975: 64-65

## III

We shall now critically look at the above position of Chomsky. First, we shall consider whether the innatist explanation of linguistic universals is the only explanation. Of course, Chomsky would think so. He would insist that it is only on the assumption that there are innate linguistic principles that "one can explain phenomena that must otherwise be regarded as accidental" (Chomsky 1967: 102-28). Strictly speaking, no other assumption about linguistic phenomena, according to Chomsky, can have any explanatory value. He argues in the following manner. All human languages have certain basic similarities, and this is a strong evidence in favour of the existence of innate linguistic universals. But he overlooks the fact that this evidence is not conclusive. He assumes that since there are linguistic universals or a common core in all natural languages, we can conclude that these linguistic universals are innately inherent in human minds. But this conclusion of Chomsky is highly dubious. There is nothing in the linguistic universals themselves which can show that these universals are innate. Chomsky may retort that he takes up basic similarities as evidence of innate linguistic universals, because no other plausible explanation is available to explain these basic similarities. If this is Chomsky's position, we may, following Putnam (1971) or Copper (1975), devise alternative theses of linguistic universals without invoking any innateness hypothesis.

We may try to show with Putnam that human languages have basic similarities among them because they have descended from a common origin. This suggestion seems plausible in view of the general belief that the human race has resulted from a single evolutionary leap, and that initially the human race was confined to an extremely small group from which it spread gradually. It goes without saying that if this is the picture of the evolution of human society, then all natural languages may be thought of as coming from a common parent language. To quote Putnam at length:

> ... it is overwhelmingly likely that all human languages are descended from a single original language, and that the existence today of what are called "unrelated" languages is accounted for by the great lapse of time and by countless

> historical changes. This is, indeed, likely ... since the human race itself is now generally believed to have resulted from a single evolutionary "leap", and since the human population was extremely small and concentrated for millennia, and only gradually spread from Asia to other continents. Thus, even if language-using was learned or invented rather than "built in", or even if only some general dispositions in the direction of language using are "built in", it is likely that some one group of humans first developed language as we know it, and then spread this through conquest or imitation to the rest of the human population. Indeed, we do know that this is just how alphabetic writing spread. In any case, I repeat, this hypothesis – a single origin for human language – is certainly required by the I.H. (Innateness Hypothesis), but much weaker than the I.H.
>
> – 1971: 136

Against Putnam, Chomsky remarks that there is no evidence for common origin. But this does not seem to have any point. This appeal to common origin is what we consider most authentic and reasonable when we find that a number of languages have similarities among them and form a significant group. There is no reason why this should not be extended from some languages to all languages, why we should not think that all languages having similarities among them have not come from a common origin. Chomsky may retort that basic similarities cannot be explained in this way. We cannot account for the basic similarities merely by saying that the structure of any natural language is "simply an accidental consequence of common descent" (Chomsky 1971: 125). His point is that any explanation in terms of common decent is ad hoc, for there is no necessary connection between the fact of common descent and the existence of linguistic universals. Is it not possible that languages have a common origin, and yet they do not have any significant similarity? If Chomsky takes this stance, this goes against his position as well. The thesis of common descent will be affected not by the possibility of languages having a common origin, and yet not having basic similarities, but only if such languages do actually exist. Now if there are really such languages which lack basic similarity, then it will disprove not only the thesis of common origin but also Chomsky's innateness hypothesis.

In addition, Cooper (1975: 162-82) makes a list of cases of linguistic universals[4] which do not invite an innatist explanation. We may deal with only some of them in order to emphasize that when one considers the communicative purposes and uses to which language is put, then it ceases to be surprising that all languages should display some similar features. These features are there, not because of some alleged innate biological wiring, but because they are natural devices for enabling certain communicative purposes. If the pragmatic dimension of language really does matter, then we can select from Cooper the following alternatives to the innalist explanation of linguistic universals: (a) all or nearly all languages have a preference for suffixing over prefixing; and (b) all languages have sentences of both active and passive forms.

a. Why this preference in all languages for suffixing over prefixing? One of the reasons is that it serves a great pragmatic role: it facilitates our learning. To explain further, we can refer with Cooper to Osgood who has amply demonstrated that learning is helped in "convergent" cases where varied stimuli elicit functionally identical responses; whereas learning is hampered in "divergent" cases where similar stimuli can give rise to different response. Now there is some analogy between "convergent" cases and stem-suffix. For example, various stimuli with the sufficer, painter, baker, driver, engineer, etc. are taken as denoting chiefly the agent or doer of a thing. On the other hand, the prefix-stem has some

[4] We have extensively used Cooper's ideas about linguistic universals.

correspondence with "divergent" cases. For example, similar stimuli with the prefix-a are taken in different senses: abed, abroad, ashore in the sense of on or in; while arise, awake or alright in the sense of *out* or *from*. Now if the prefix-stem corresponds to "divergent" cases and stem-suffix to "convergent" cases, it is no wonder that languages should have preference for suffix over prefix in the interest of learning. Besides – what is equally crucial – there are also communicative reasons. We know that the stem has greater communicative force and hence will tend to be positional first. Thus, if in a telegram the affixes are left out, we can understand the message in some way. But the task will be hopeless if the stem is left out in the telegram. Similarly, in the more technical language of information theory, there is greater stress on stem to decode the message. This is because the stem eliminates the possibility of varied responses. It is just on this ground that we can argue for our preferring suffix to prefix.

b. This is also derived from the general inclination that people have while engaging in discourse. When we talk about things, we usually want to highlight one thing over another according to what we consider urgent. Given this general human propensity or inclination, it is not surprising that languages should have active and passive forms. If we are concerned with or interested in the agent who has carried out an action, we use an active form, e.g. John opens the door. But if we are more concerned with or interested in the object that is performed by an agent, the device for encoding this preference is the passive form, e.g. the door is opened by John. In other words, given communicative purposes should we expect, that we would have different ways of saying the same thing in the active or the passive – according to what object we are directing the hearer's attention?

c. An even more important example, perhaps, is the following. According to Chomsky, all languages – at least at the deep level – have a subject–predicate structure, which he puts down to innate wiring, because it is derived from the universal grammar that one innately possesses. We might have raised here the problem, whether universal grammar or some basic structural principles that accommodate only the rigid or bound NP-VP form or subject – predicate form will not fail to explain language like Latin or Sanskrit containing free word-order. In fact, Chomsky himself was aware of this problem. In his conversations with Mitson Ronat under the title, *Language and Responsibility* (1977), he holds that Ken Hale has studied Walbiri language and has found that this language consists of a relatively free word-order. But he leaves this problem unresolved. We should not, however, press this problem further, for our fundamental aim is to show that subject – predicate form which Chomsky puts down to innate wiring can be explained otherwise. This is what Strawson has pointed out in his *Individuals* and *Subject and Predicate in Logic and Grammar.* He has argued, plausibly, that any language which can efficiently perform the central task of language – that of making claims about things, of describing how things are – is bound to favour something like the subject–predicate form. To take one example (Strawson 1974: 106), in describing a situation, say, the disorder of a room, and how things are there, we use subject–predicate sentences like, A chair was overturned; A bottle was lying on the floor; A picture was broken. Now in the subject-position, we have certain concrete particulars which can be identified, re-identified as items of our experience. No doubt, "chair", "bottle" or "picture" are kind-identifying terms. Yet we can identify, re-identify spatio-temporal instances of them. The verb phrases in the predicate in all the above sentences are neither kind identifying, nor individually identifying terms; they state the conditions the concrete particulars are in. In this way, we capture things and how they are in the subject–predicate form.

Two points are involved in (a) to (c):

(i) there may be perfectly plausible explanations of linguistic universals other than in terms of innate language-specific mechanisms; and

(ii) those explanations are in terms of the pragmatic aspects of language – the use of language to conduct our interpersonal communicative purposes.

The credentials of innatist explanation of linguistic universals are also suspect on another ground. We have already considered structure-dependent rule, and how Chomsky gives it an innatist flavour. He holds that if a child speaks English, this does not mean that the child knows its grammar innately. For if it did, it would have great problem in speaking Spanish, if its parents moved to Spain during its very early age. In fact, the child can speak any language – whether English or Spanish – because it knows and innately employs those principles and categories (structure-dependence, for example) from which all the languages – English, Spanish, etc. – are derived. Or, to put the same thing in a different way, all the speakers of the world are involved in fundamentally similar activities (employing rules, etc.) which belong to men's innate equipment. But we do not understand why we should agree with Chomsky on this point. It may be admitted that when we form interrogatives from indicative sentences, there is structure-dependent rule behind it. But it is unclear as to why this structure-dependent rule should call forth deeper innatist explanation. Strictly speaking, all that a structure-dependent rule shows is what we normally and naturally do. When we transform the indicative, e.g. "The old woman is happy" into the interrogative "Is the old woman happy?". We keep intact "the old woman". And this is most natural. We want to retain the phrase referring to what we are interested in (the old woman), no matter whether we say something about her or ask about her. There is nothing surprising in it to compel any innatist explanation.

We can doubt any innatist explanation from another consideration also. A little probe will reveal that there can be alternative grammars of a language. Each grammar can pick up certain features, and can claim that these characterize the grammars of all languages. Consequently, we have alternative linguistic universals. Now which of them we accept will not be determined objectively; it will depend on what grammar we opt for. Suppose, we accept Chomsky's transformational grammar of English. Then our paradigm will be subject, defined as left most *NP* in the underlying structure, and we shall try to incorporate subject in all languages. We shall not be hemmed in even if we do not discover subjects in a language. We shall try to emphasize, they have just been deleted in the surface level, but they are in the deep level. On the other hand, if we accept Fillmore's case grammar of English where the verb occupies the pivotal position, we shall not regard as basic the subject–predicate construction. We shall focus on case relations, e.g. between Agentives and Locatives, with categories like subject being treated as derivative.

If the foregoing argument is true, then the moral is against the prospect of an innatist explanation. For what will count as linguistic universals will be a matter of our choice, what grammar we prefer. This implies that linguistic universals cannot be innate. For what is innate cannot depend on our choice.

From the above analysis, we arrive at a closely related point to argue, with Devitt and Sterelny (1987: 154), against Chomsky:

> ... the common features may be artefacts of the method theorists use to construct grammars, rather than indications

of what is common to the grammars actually internalized by speakers.

We think that this observation of Devitt and Sterelny highlights two important points:

(a) Linguistic universals may be artefacts of linguistic theory. In other words, from the fact that a linguist may employ the same categories, principles, etc. in his descriptions of all languages, it will not follow that these languages are really governed by such principles, i.e. that speakers of all those languages have internalized just those principles. (After all, one might describe bee behaviour in terms of game theory; but it hardly follows that bees know the principles of game theory).

(b) There is really something question-begging in Chomsky's account. One of his reasons for holding there is innate knowledge of *X*, *Y*, etc., is that *X*, *Y*, etc. are universal features of language. But in order to establish that these are genuinely universal features, and not theorists' artefacts, he needs to assume that they are part of our innate equipment. Now what could justify that assumption? Only perhaps the claim that all speakers internalize the principles, etc. of the best, simplest linguistic theory, as propounded by transformational generative (TG) grammar of Chomsky. But why make this claim? Does it not sound dogmatic just like the theological claim that the world must act in accordance with the simplest, ideal physical theory as sponsored by it?

## IV

Let us now return to the main arguments that Chomsky gives to support his innateness hypothesis – the ones from complexity and poverty of stimuli. First, let us deal with his complexity argument. We have already pointed out that Chomsky stresses the complexity of language in order to argue for innate learning mechanism of the child. But complexity is, after all, a function of how something is described. Let us, for example, take the sentence, "He rode his bicycle along the road". Now if we like, we can give it a very complicated paraphrase.

> He moved the muscles of his legs in such a way that he propelled a machine with the following properties ... in such a way as to maintain equilibrium between gravitational forces and ... etc. ...

Hence, whether anything will look enormously complex will depend on how we prefer to describe it. Similarly, the ability to, say, convert an active sentence into a passive one can be made to sound a very complicated business – if we prefer to describe it in terms of technical linguistics. Then we shall have to say the following. The element passive (optional) is generated by the PS rules lying at the base. The element passive, however, triggers off obligatory and phonemic rules to give shape to the final sentence. Thus, $NP_1$ + Aux + $NP_2$ + by + passive → $NP_2$ + Aux + be + en + V + en + by + $NP_1$: The boy has been seen by the man. Obviously, to turn an active sentence into a passive one will sound like a remarkably complex operation, if we describe it in the terms of technical linguistics (Chomsky's transformational generative grammar). But described simply, as turning an active sentence into a passive, one, it does not sound like a complex operation. Of course, if we equate knowing how to convert the sentence with unconscious propositional knowledge of some very complicated rule, then we guarantee that the capacity to make the conversion is very complex one. But if arguments against unconscious knowledge are right, it is illegitimate to make that equation. In other words, Chomsky can only claim that our linguistic understanding is something highly complex if we already accept his account of understanding in terms of propositional grasp of rules. This is what we do not accept.

Next, let us look at Chomsky's poverty of the stimulus argument. Chomsky treats the data available to the child in a very restricted way – as mere sounds from which the child must infer to the system of rules of the language he is learning. This is questionable for at least two reasons:

(a) If we take lessons from Wiggins (1997), McDowell (1984) and Heidegger (1980), it is implausible to suppose that we go through a process (ordinarily) of inferring meanings from raw acoustic data. This is like supposing we recognize people's moods from the raw data of facial movements, etc. Wiggins, McDowell or Heidegger want to emphasize that we directly experience or perceive meaning, structure, etc. in people's speech, which is a "social object". We hear someone describing something, not just producing sounds. We may substantiate it with reference to Heidegger. Heidegger's model is a description of hearing:

> What we first hear is never noises or complexes of sounds, but the creaking wagon, the motorcycle. It requires a very artificial and complicated frame of mind to "hear" a "pure noise". The fact that motorcycles and wagons are what we proximally hear is the phenomenal evidence that in every case Dasein, as being-in-the-world, already dwells amidst what is available within-the-world; it certainly does not dwell primarily amidst "sensations". – Dreyfus 1995: 218

If we apply it to language, it will mean that we do not hear only meaningless sounds, only "acoustic blasts", and then posit mental rules and representations to interpret them. As Heidegger puts it:

> When we are explicitly hearing the telling of another, we immediately understand what is said, or – to put it more exactly we are already with him, in advance, among the entities which the telling is about ... what we primarily do not hear is the pronunciation of sounds.
> – Ibid.: 219

The point made by Heidegger is that, phenomenologically, language is used in a shared context and as long as we dwell in a community's practices, we hear words as already meaningful, and not as mere sounds. We perceive and experience words as already "supplied with significations" (ibid.). Therefore, if we unduly restrict what can be said to be perceptually and experimentally available to a person, it is easy to make it appear as if this is much too impoverished a basis from which to infer what sentences mean, etc. so that we then need to bring in something like innate understanding to bridge the gap. But may be the problem is with that restriction.

(b) It follows from the above argument that when Chomsky discusses the situation of the child learner, he makes it sound, wrongly, as if the child has nothing to go on except mere noises which might, as it were, issue from a tape recorder. In fact, the child learns from other people in actual situation, where the context enables the learning process. The child observes the linguistic behaviour going on around it, and the corresponding response pattern of the elders. Thus, when the child hears someone saying, "Bring the cow", he notices the response of the individual to whom the sentence is addressed. Again, he hears the sentence, "Bind the cow" and notices the corresponding action of his elders. In this way, the child's learning a language in interpersonal context goes on. What we are trying to insist on is that once we take into account the whole of what is impinging on the learner – not just the mere noises showering on him – it is unclear why we should speak of the poverty of the stimuli available to him. Once again, it seems, Chomsky's account suffers from ignoring or playing down the role of the social or interpersonal in language learning.

A similar way to substantiate the contention that language acquisition is a part of socialization is this. If we abide by the dictate of modulary thesis of language, then there is the following consequence. The processes which are responsible for the acquisition, understanding and production of language are quite independent of the processes that are responsible for general cognition and learning. A certain level of cognitive ability is, indeed, essential for playing chess, for example. But we all learn a language and this does not involve cognitive ability of the sort required to learn how to play chess. That is why everyone can learn his native language, while everyone does not solve puzzles or prove theorems. "But", as Putnam has significantly pointed out, "everyone does learn pattern recognition, automobile driving, and everyone in fact can solve many problems that no computer can solve" (1971: 138).

So why should one assume that the principles underlying the acquisition of language are likely to be special to the domain of language? Does it not sound more plausible that we acquire language by general learning principles of the sort that enable us to learn automobile driving, solve problems, play chess or something like that? This point, incidentally, is also made by connectionists like Elman and his colleagues (1996) when they say, "a domain-general pattern recognition device would suffice", i.e. language acquisition can be taken care of by an undifferentiated neural network that suffices for everything, including vision, face recognition and the like. Being a part of general learning strategy, learning of language needs sonic extra-linguistic information. This is provided for the learner by the appropriate behaviour, practices of his linguistic community in the context of a form of life shared by the community.

# 6

# Concluding Survey

Now we may look back to give a brief sketch of the preceding chapters where the general direction of our argument is towards the centrality of the social and interpersonal in any account of linguistic knowledge. In Chapter 1, we have introduced the fundamental points of Chomsky's mentalistic account of language. What he intends to drive home may be divided into two parts:

(a) According to him, the goal of any linguistic theory is to account for "creativity of language", i.e. the speaker's ability to produce new sentences – sentences which can be understood by others though they do not correspond to sentences which are familiar. Now the thesis by which he explains this creativity is that of competence. It is due to our having competence that we can produce and understand sentences not encountered before. Thus, the notion of competence plays a vital role in Chomsky. This notion shows Chomsky's bias towards the mental, since it means that linguistic rules are mentally represented or that we have unconscious knowledge of language. And most importantly this notion of competence enables Chomsky to do justice to the crucial fact of creativity.

(b) He also appeals to innateness hypothesis in terms of

linguistic universals to endorse his idea of competences or knowledge of language.

In Chapters 2-4 we have taken up

(a) Chomsky's understanding of competence in more detail, and

(b) In Chapter 5 we have considered, the relevance of the innateness hypothesis in the context of his thesis of knowledge of language.

In Chapter 2 we have tried to understand Chomsky's account of "competence" in connection with "performance" and "creativity", showing some shifts and inconsistencies involved here. Chomsky uses the word, "competence" not in the usual sense or as Ryle or Hymes would understand it, i.e. in the sense of ability. He insists on a distinction between competence or what the speaker of a language knows unconsciously and performance or what he is able to do or does in the actual context. We have, however, expressed doubt about the feasibility of his notion of competence as distinct from our everyday one which he would regard as non-linguistic knowledge (know how).

Chomsky, of course, would not deny that there is relation between competence and performance in spite of distinction between them. In fact, he makes it a point to show that competence in his sense explains appropriate performance. But if our normal sense of competence has any plausibility, to explain performance in terms of competence seems empty.

We also notice some shift or inconsistency in his endeavour to explain creativity in terms of competence, where he seems to veer between talking about creativity as a matter, simply, of recognizing and understanding new sentences, and as a matter of actual use in context, etc. Consequently, two other relations between performance and competence follow:

(i) performance is evidence for competence; and

(ii) performance is the criterion for competence.

But if (ii) is taken seriously, it goes against or disrupts Chomsky's official stand, viz. that competence is conceptually divorced from actual use in context, etc. from communicative intentional understanding. Of course, it may be thought that all such disruption is due to Chomsky's careless use of expression, and that despite all shift and uncertainties in his way of speaking, he really wishes to confine linguistic knowledge to something abstracted from actual use in context, etc. from communication intention. But then our point is whether this abstraction can be made or nor?

In Chapters 3 and 4 we have tried to look more closely into the specific content of his thought about knowledge of language.

In Chapter 3 we have tried to ascertain why knowledge of language, according to Chomsky, is unconscious and whether such tacit knowledge makes any sense. In this connection, we have also considered some possibilities that can cover the kind of knowledge postulated by Chomsky. But the sum and substance of our argument is that no plausible sense can be made of Chomsky's alleged knowledge of language.

Particularly in Chapter 4 we have considered a very crucial implication of Chomsky's knowledge of language. It is that his account of knowledge of language involves privacy. His contention is that it is both loose and theoretically unhelpful to speak of people speaking the "same" language. Strictly speaking, each speaker knows a different language though these different languages may resemble one another closely. There is no such thing as the English language; there is only a class of resembling languages (mine, John's or Mary's). If this is so, then we cannot appeal to the English language in describing or explaining or analysing what it is for one to know the rules of one's language. From this follows two things:

(i) there is no socially shared public language; and

(ii) each speaker follows rules which are unique to him.

To put our point against (i) we have mainly followed Wiggins. If Wiggins is right, no account can be given of what it is to know a language which does not refer to a shared public language. Strictly speaking, someone who knows a language knows a particular public language. If there is my language or your language or his language, then there can be no communication and no objective basis for judging that such and such utterance is correct or incorrect, apt or inept. Against (ii) we have followed Wittgenstein or Kripke's interpretation to vindicate that the very notion of rule requires a reference to commonly agreed practices which determine how the rule is applied and what the rule amounts to. Our reactions against (i) and (ii) will perhaps highlight the general line of criticism we want to take against Chomsky. It is this. His account of competence, knowledge of language ignores a social, interpersonal dimension.

But Chomsky may defend the privacy of knowledge of language by his well-known innateness hypothesis. This is what we have considered in Chapter 5. The role of innateness hypothesis may be understood in two ways:

(i) This hypothesis can reinforce Chomsky's emphasis on privacy or the "asocial". For, according to this hypothesis to acquire knowledge of a particular language, a child must already possess knowledge of principles and categories of universal grammar. Now if there is such innate knowledge, it must be the one that the child will possess independently of and prior to its relation with other speakers. If so, why should we not think that knowledge of one's language is private and independent of communal participation?

(ii) This hypothesis also explains how linguistic competence is possible.

(i) and (ii) will make it clear how vital innateness hypothesis is for Chomsky. But this hypothesis seems highly dubious.

Chomsky talks about innate linguistic universals which account for our competence or knowledge of language. This innateness claim depends crucially on two considerations:

(a) the child's ability to master a very complex within a short span; and

(b) its ability to pick up its language in spite of the poverty of the stimulus.

Against the idea of innate linguistic universals, our point is that given the communicative purposes and uses of language, it seems very reasonable that all languages should have some common features. These features are there not because of some innate wiring, but because they are natural devices appropriate for communicative purposes. Against the complexity argument, our point is that whether language looks complex is a function of how we describe it. Again, our linguistic understanding will be highly complex if we already accept Chomsky's account of understanding in terms of unconscious grasp of rules. But we have already argued in Chapter 3 that such unconscious knowledge is not intelligible. Against the poverty of the stimulus argument our point is that this argument works only if we take the data available to the child in a very restricted sense – as mere sounds from which the child interprets the system of rules of its language. But, as Wiggins, McDowell or Heidegger would point out; we do not encounter merely "acoustic blasts" but directly experience meaning, structure, etc. in peoples' speech which is a "social object". It is not that the child hears nothing but meaningless sounds, and then infers from them rules of the language he is learning. In fact, the child learns by dwelling in the community practices and language comes to it not as sounds as if from a tape-recorder but as already being infused with significations. Hence, by restricting the data to mere noises, Chomsky overlooks the social or interpersonal role in language learning.

# Appendix

INCIDENTALLY, this innateness hypothesis of Chomsky reminds us of the seventeenth-century rationalists, especially Descartes and Leibnitz, with whom he acknowledges his very close affinity. For example, in his "Recent Contributions to the Theory of Innate Ideas" (1974), he remarks that "contemporary research supports a theory of psychological a priori principles that bears a striking resemblance to the classical doctrine of innate ideas". But it seems that Chomsky exaggerates the degree of affinity between his and the seventeenth-century position. Indeed, both Descartes and Leibnitz claimed that there are innate ideas, and Chomsky has revived those ideas for his psycho-linguistics. But strictly speaking, this should be taken with reservation.

Let us first take the case of Descartes. According to him, there are some ideas or concepts (e.g. the idea of a triangle or the idea of perfection or the idea of God) which were not, nor could have been acquired through experience. He argues in the following way. Never can we draw nor have we seen a perfect or ideal triangle. All we can say is that the particular triangles we draw or see are approximations to the ideal triangle. The question is, why we consider the particular samples as approximations to the ideal triangle that we have never experienced. This is possible only because we have the innate idea of a triangle. This is how Descartes has developed his theory of innate ideas, and C. Travis has identified Descartes' theory as the weaker thesis of innate ideas. Let us now see how Chomsky utilizes the thesis of Descartes. He agrees with Descartes in taking the "cognitive power" to be a faculty that is properly called mind which is not "completely under the control of sense or imagination or memory". But at the same time, there are important differences between them. According to Descartes, mind is totally independent of body, and innate ideas belong to or are properties of the mind. Chomsky, of course, refers to the mind in the context of innate ideas, but he interprets mind in biological and genetic terms. Again, Descartes indeed claimed that we have innate ideas, say, idea of a triangle, etc. But nowhere had he claimed that the syntax of natural language is innate. On the contrary, he seems to have emphasized that though concepts are innate, language is quite arbitrary, that we arbitrarily assign, in the words of Searle, "Verbal labels to an innate system of concepts". Further, Descartes will not accept the possibility of unconscious knowledge which, as we have already seen, constitutes the basic theme of Chomsky's system.

Leibnitz equally claimed that we have innate ideas. But he puts his position, as C. Travis tells us, "in the stronger sense". He holds that unless we have innate ideas, particularly those of truth and identity, experience could not teach us anything. If I do not know already that contradictions cannot be true, experience cannot teach us, for example that "a hawk is not a handsaw". It is true that we can say that hawks fly, but not handsaws. But that may just mean: hawks/handsaws fly and do not. Thus, if we have to learn from experience, the mandate must come from our innate logical competence. Chomsky appears to come closer to Leibnitz. Like Leibnitz, he is equally concerned with a specific competence, i.e. linguistic competence. His idea is that a child cannot learn a language by being simply exposed to the linguistic community around it without having innate grammatical competence. Yet Chomsky's position will be something different. Leibnitz looks at innate ideas as inclinations or dispositions.

To quote his words:

> ... it is that ideas and truths are for us innate as inclinations, dispositions, habits, or natural potentialities, and not as

> actions, although these potentialities are always accompanied by some actions, often insensible, which correspond to them.

Thus, the contention of Leibnitz will be that we are innately disposed to learn from experience. But Chomsky cannot merely say that human beings are innately predisposed to speak or learn from experience, that linguistic data, when given, will put innate disposition into action and consequently we learn a language. This will indeed be a trivial, or in the words of Devitt and Sterelny, "boring thesis". This contention will be boring or trivial, because every informed person, even the staunch empiricist should not object to it. For, otherwise we cannot explain why lions cannot talk or learn language. What, in fact, has made Chomsky's innateness hypothesis "interesting" or "exciting" is the contention that human beings have an innate, richly structured, language specific, learning device that enables the child to come up with the right grammar on the basis of its exposure to the language or linguistic data around it.

If the foregoing is well taken we should take Chomsky's affinity with the seventeenth-century rationalist very cautiously and can now write more about Chomsky's specific thesis of innateness.

# Bibliography


Bloomfield, L., 1935, *Language*, London: George Allen & Unwin.

Chomsky, Noam, 1964, "Current Issues in Linguistic Theory", in *The Structure of Language*, ed. J.A. Fodor and J.J, Katz, Englewood Cliffs, NJ: Prentice-Hall.

———, 1966, "Topics in the Theory of Generative Grammar", in *Current Trends in Linguistics*, ed. T.A. Sebeok, vol. III, The Hague: Moutan.

———, 1967, "Some General Properties of Phonological Rules", *Language*, 43: 102-28, London: George Allen & Unwin.

———, 1968, *Language and Mind*, New York: Harcourt, Brace & World.

———, 1969, "Linguistics and Philosophy", in *Language and Philosophy*, ed. S. Hook, New York: New York University Press.

———, 1972, *Language and Mind*, enlarged edn, New York: Harcourt Brace Jonanovich.

———, 1974, "Recent Contributions to the Theory of Innate Ideas", in *The Philosophy of Language*, ed. J.R. Searle, London: Oxford University Press.

———, 1976, *Reflections on Language*, Fontana, CA: Random House.

———, 1977, *Language and Responsibility*, New York: Pantheon Books.

———, 1980, *Rules and Representations*, Oxford: Basil Blackwell.

———, 1988, *Language and Problems of Knowledge*, Cambridge, MA: MIT Press.

———, 1990, "On the Nature, Use and Acquisition of Language", in *Mind and Cognition: A Reader*, ed. W.G. Lycan, Oxford: Basil Blackwell.

———, 1995, "Language and Nature", *Mind*, 104 (January).

———, 2000, *New Horizons in the Study of Language and Mind,* Cambridge: Cambridge University Press.

Cooper, D.E., 1975, *Knowledge of Language,* London: Prism Press and New York: Humanities Press.

D'Agostino, F., 1986, *Chomsky's System of Ideas,* Oxford: Clarendon Press.

Devitt, M. and Kim Sterelny, 1987, *Language and Reality: An Introduction to the Philosophy of Language,* Oxford: Basil Blackwell.

Dreyfus, H.L., 1995, *Being-in-the-World: A Commentary on Heidegger's Being and Time,* Cambridge, MA: MIT Press.

Elman, J., et al., 1996, *Rethinking Innateness: A Connectionist Perspective on Development,* Cambridge, MA: MIT Press.

Fodor, J., 1975, *The Language of Thought,* New York: Crowell.

Foster, Cf. John, 1976, "Meaning and Truth Theory", in *Truth and Meaning: Essays in Semantics,* ed. Gareth Evans and John McDowell, Oxford: University Press.

Grayling, A.C., 1988, *Wittgenstein,* Oxford: Oxford University Press.

Harman, Gilbert, 1971, "Psychological Aspects of the Theory of Syntax", in *Readings in the Philosophy of Language,* eds. J.F. Rosenberg and C. Travis, Englewood Cliffs, NJ: Prentice-Hall.

———, (ed.), 1974, *On Noam Chomsky: Critical Essays,* New York: Anchor Books.

Heidegger, M., 1980, *Being and Time,* tr. J. Macquarrie and E. Robinson, Oxford: Blackwell.

Hook, Sydney (ed.), 1969, *Language and Philosophy: A Symposium,* New York: New York University Press.

Hymes, D.H., 1979, "On Communicative Competence", in *Sociolinguistics,* ed. J.B. Pride and J. Holmes, London: Penguin.

Kripke, S., 1982, *Wittgenstein on Rules and Private Language,* Oxford: Basil Blackwell.

———, 1977, *Language and Responsibility,* New York: Panthan Book.

Lyons, John, 1990, *Noam Chomsky,* London: Fontana.

Merleau-Ponty, M., 1967, *Phenomenology of Perception*, tr. Colin Smith, London: Routledge & Kegan Paul.

———, 1982, "On the Phenomenology of Language", quoted from Herbert Spiegelberg, *The Phenomenological Movement*, The Hague: Martinus Nijhoff.

McDowell, John, 1984 "Wittgenstein on Following a Rule", *Synthese*, 58.

McGinn, Colin, 1984, *Wittgenstein on Meaning*, Oxford: Basil Blackwell.

Putnam, H., 1971, "The Innateness Hypothesis and Explanatory Models in Linguistics", in *Philosophy of Language*, ed. J.R. Searle, Oxford: Oxford University Press.

Quine, W.V., 1960, *Word and Object*, Cambridge, MA: MIT Press.

Ramsey, William and Stich Stephen, 1990, "Connectionism and Three Levels of Nativism", *Synthese*, 82(2): 177-205.

Ryle, Gilbert, 1980, *The Concept of Mind*, London: Penguin Books.

Searle, J.R., 1970, *Speech Acts*, London: Cambridge University Press.

——— (ed.), 1971, *Philosophy of Language*, Oxford: Oxford University Press.

———, 1974, "Chomsky's Revolution in Linguistics", in *On Noam Chomsky: Critical Essays*, ed. Gilbert Harman, New York: Anchor Books.

Smith, Neil, 1999, *Chomsky: Ideas and Ideals*, Cambridge: Cambridge University Press.

Stich, S.P., 1972, "Grammar, Psychology and Indeterminacy", *Journal of Philosophy*, 69: 799-818.

Strawson, P.F., 1974, *Subject and Predicate in Logic and Grammar*, London: Methuen.

———, 2012, "Meaning and Truth", in *The Philosophy of Language*, ed. A.P. Martinich, Oxford: Oxford University Press.

Wiggins, David, 1997, "Languages as Social Objects", *Philosophy*, 72: 499-525.

Wittgenstein, L., 1953, *Philosophycal Investigations*, tr. G.E.M. Anscombe, 3rd edn, London: Pearson.

Wright, Crispin, 1986/1991, *Realism, Meaning and Truth*, Oxford: Basil Blackwell.

# Index